P9-CLZ-180

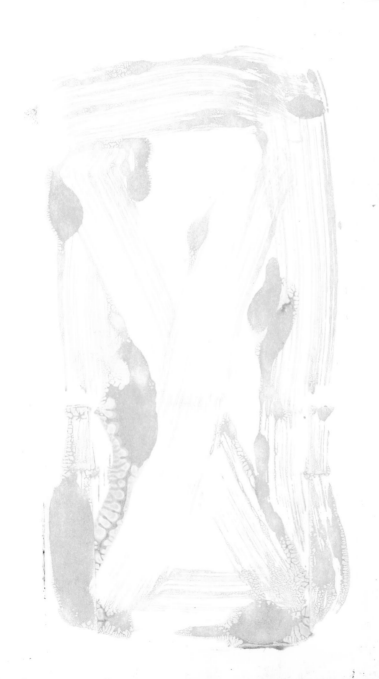

Andrew Jackson
and
The Battle of New Orleans

About the Book

The Battle of New Orleans was the final act in a drama that began long before it was fought. When General Andrew Jackson led his soldiers against the Creek Indians under Red Eagle, he knew that the enemy basically was the British, who had armed the Creeks and set them against the American frontier settlements. Dee Brown, author of *Bury My Heart at Wounded Knee,* begins his vivid historical account with the Battle of Horseshoe Bend between Creeks and white Americans. Dramatic events lead one with a sense of mounting excitement to the climax—the last battle fought between British and Americans.

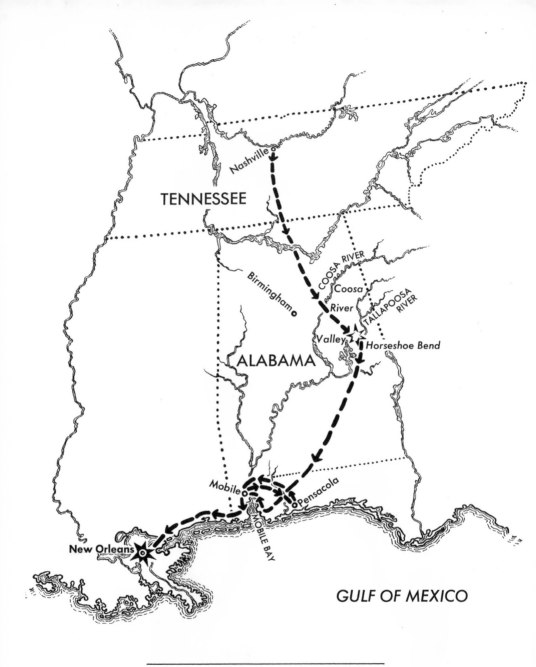

The Battle of New Orleans

AMERICAN BATTLES AND CAMPAIGNS

EARL SCHENCK MIERS
GENERAL EDITOR

Andrew Jackson
and The Battle of
New Orleans

1

by Dee Brown

G. P. Putnam's Sons  New York

FOUNDED 1838

GPPS

Contents

Note

Instances of direct dialogue in this book have been reconstructed from historical reports of the period.

The Author

1

Horseshoe Bend
and Red Eagle

A flaming arrow streaked out of the pale sky into the
midst of the encampment. Rifles crackled on the right,
and ghostly forms of pickets came running in from the
pine trees.

General Andrew Jackson flung the blanket off his
shoulders and leaned forward. "They've attacked us on
the right," he said calmly. "So the main body must be
on the left. Weatherford's Red Sticks fight like their
British teachers." He stood up, buttoned his blouse, and
started toward his saddled horse. "Captain Reid, tell
Colonel Coffee to clear out those skirmishers while I
form my Tennesseans for a charge on the left."

"Yes, sir." Captain John Reid mounted quickly and
spurred his horse into a gallop. As he sped across the
clearing he wondered how Andy Jackson always
seemed to know when and where the Creek Indians
would attack. An hour earlier the general had waked
him in pitch-black darkness, and they had been sitting
on their blankets, sipping cold tea and waiting to be
surprised.

It had been like that since the campaign began in

October, 1813, after the Creeks massacred two hundred and fifty settlers at Fort Mims. "The British are the real enemy," Andrew Jackson told his men. "Through 1812 they fought us from Canada, but soon they will attack us from the South. They've armed the Creeks and set them against us. To get at the British we must defeat the Creeks, and the Creeks will not be beaten until we kill or capture their leader, Red Eagle."

Red Eagle's real name was William Weatherford, a man whose ancestors were French, Scottish, and Creek. Through the winter Jackson had led his men down from Tennessee into the Coosa River valley to fight six hard battles with Red Eagle Weatherford's warriors. Now it was March, 1814, and Red Eagle had not yet been defeated.

As Captain Reid neared Colonel John Coffee's brushwood headquarters, the dawn sky was brightening. Musket fire exploded suddenly on his front, dotting the forest with flashes of orange. He found Coffee on horseback near the woods line and gave him General Jackson's message.

"A company of mounted riflemen are in there now," Coffee said. "At first it was so dark they could see nothing but muzzle flashes to fire at, but they're driving the Creeks hard now. If Old Hickory Jackson needs support, I can spare my reserves."

Old Hickory's Tennessee foot soldiers needed no help that day. Firing volleys from their long rifles, they charged the woods and broke up a barrage of Red Stick musketry and arrows. By the time Colonel Coffee and Captain Reid arrived with the reserve company only scattered firing could be heard from the forest. General Jackson, brandishing his sword angrily, rode out of the trees. "If Weatherford would only stand and fight, we'd end this infernal Creek War!" One of the infantrymen suddenly raised a rifle. "Hold your fire!" the general cried.

An Indian appeared suddenly from behind a nearby tree. "He's a friendly," Jackson growled. "Can't you see he's wearing a deer tail in his hair?"

"He's the Coosa Creek you sent south, sir," Captain Reid said.

"He picked a bad time to come back in," Jackson replied as he dismounted. "But maybe he can tell us where Weatherford is." He motioned to the others to remain where they were and began walking in long strides toward the Indian.

For several minutes the general and the Creek talked, the Indian gesturing often in sign language. Then, as abruptly as he had come, the Creek turned and vanished into the woods.

When Jackson returned, his steel-blue eyes were unusually bright. "Colonel Coffee," he said, "I want you to send your spy company to scout the Horseshoe Bend of Tallapoosa River. Davy Crockett and his sharpshooters will go with them. They may find Weatherford there with a thousand Red Sticks behind fortifications. Captain Reid, you will start a courier off to the Thirty-ninth Infantry with orders to Colonel Williams to join us there. Williams' Regulars have been spoiling for a fight, and now they'll have one. We'll break camp and march out within the hour."

At dawn of March 27, Jackson's field army of two thousand men was in position on both sides of Horseshoe Bend. With his aide, Captain Reid, the general went forward to examine the Bend's defenses. He saw that the river made almost a complete circle, leaving a large peninsula surrounded on three sides by water. Across the narrow neck of land, the Red Sticks had used pine logs to build a rampart eight feet high. Upper and lower ranges of portholes for rifle fire were cut into the rampart, and it curved to the center so that an attacking force would meet a withering cross fire from two levels.

"British engineering," Jackson declared with admiration. "It won't be easy for us to break through that wall."

"They've also felled trees along the riverbank," Reid said.

Behind the barrier, hundreds of Creek warriors moved among clusters of fortified log houses. Their prophets, or medicine men, were summoning them to battle with jingling bells. The prophets' faces were painted black, and their heads and shoulders were covered with feathers. Before each group of houses stood a pole painted bright red, the red sticks of war which gave these hostile Creeks their name.

"We'll bring up our two artillery pieces," Jackson said, "and show Weatherford the power of cannonballs."

By midmorning the guns were in position on a low hill less than a hundred yards from the center of the rampart. When the gunners opened fire, the slap of explosions rolled back in echoes from the woods. Inside the fortifications, Creek sharpshooters tried to pick off the artillerymen, and Jackson ordered the Thirty-ninth Regulars forward to furnish covering fire.

For two hours the cannons pounded away, but most of the balls sank harmlessly into the soft green pine logs. Between firings, the Red Stick warriors shouted mocking cries, daring the soldiers to come down and fight them.

At noontime, Jackson stopped the firing and summoned his officers for a council of war. "Our guns are too light to batter down those logs," he said. "We'll have to carry the breastwork by storm." The Thirty-ninth Regulars would lead the charge. Jackson's Tennesseans would support them. Coffee's Volunteers would guard the riverbanks to prevent them from escaping by water.

In a few minutes drummers were beating the long roll. The Regulars formed in line front, the lieutenants and sergeants in wide-belted blue uniforms taking positions with their units. A major wearing a bicorn hat, long-tailed jacket, skin-tight trousers, and black knee boots raised his sword. The drummers stopped their roll. Shouted commands swept along the line: "Fix bayonets!" "Prime and load!" "Forward—march!" The blue line moved out, increasing step to double time, and then the men were running, their bayoneted muskets glinting in the sun.

From the portholes the Creeks opened a murderous fire. All along the line men began falling, but a second line swept forward in support. In a few minutes powder smoke was so thick around the rampart that General Jackson could not see how the fighting was going. He spurred his horse forward. The smoke cleared for a moment, and he could see his men firing through the portholes, muzzle to muzzle with the defending Creeks. He saw a young lieutenant lead a charge over the logs, with a full platoon scrambling after him. "That crazy Sam Houston," Jackson muttered to himself and then

11

turned in his saddle, shouting to his Tennesseans to bring up axes and break an opening through the rampart.

A few minutes later the general rode into the Creek fort. Dozens of small fights were continuing around the houses and in ditches and undergrowth. Arrows and bullets filled the air, and in hand-to-hand fighting the desperate Creeks used spears, tomahawks and knives.

With a clatter of hooves, Captain Reid came up to report on the battle's progress outside the fort. "Colonel Coffee's men have trapped the Red Sticks in the river, sir," Reid shouted. "There's no escape for them!"

"They're beaten," Jackson replied. "Let's give them a chance to surrender."

Half an hour passed before the fighting could be broken off. The soldiers pulled back to the rampart, and Jackson sent a messenger and an interpreter forward under a truce flag.

"They'll never surrender," a voice called out, and Jackson turned to stare at Lieutenant Sam Houston. Houston's tight trousers were streaked with blood. "I offered to spare the lives of several warriors," Houston explained, "but they fought on like madmen."

"You're wounded, Lieutenant," Jackson said gruffly. "Get back to the surgeon."

Houston hobbled away but had not gone a dozen yards before the truce messengers returned. They reported that the Red Sticks refused the surrender offer.

"Did you talk with Weatherford?" Jackson asked.

"No, sir. The village chief said Weatherford was across the river."

12

Jackson frowned. "I shall not risk the lives of more of my men by attacking their fortified houses. We'll burn them out. Captain Reid, order Colonel Coffee's company of Cherokees brought forward to prepare flaming arrows."

It was a bad afternoon for the Red Sticks at Horseshoe Bend. Driven out of their burning houses, they retreated into ravines or tried to swim the river under fire of the Tennessee Volunteers. Several warriors took cover in a small redoubt of green logs which would not burn, and a party of Regulars volunteered to storm it. As Jackson watched the furious charge he was startled to see young Sam Houston leading the attack. A few minutes later the fight was over and Jackson hurried forward. He found Lieutenant Houston lying on the ground with two new wounds. "Get him on a stretcher," Jackson ordered harshly. "If he lives, that wild Sam Houston is going to make his mark in this world."

Until sundown small outbreaks of fighting continued, and then the Battle of Horseshoe Bend came to an end. Not until the next morning was Captain Reid able to collect a full list of casualties. "We lost forty-nine killed and one hundred and fifty-seven wounded," Reid reported. "Our men counted five hundred and fifty-seven dead Red Sticks and Colonel Coffee estimates at least two hundred more hit and swept away in the river."

"Weatherford, the Red Eagle? Was he among them?" the general asked.

"Our friendly Creeks searched in vain for Weatherford. No trace, sir. They've heard rumors he's rallying survivors on their sacred Hickory Ground. They believe no enemy can harm them there."

13

Jackson's long jaw clapped shut like a bear trap. "We'll march at once for the Hickory Ground," he said.

But if Weatherford was there, he fled at the army's approach, and Jackson led his men on to abandoned Fort Toulouse, raising the United States flag above it.

A few days later Captain Reid entered Jackson's headquarters to inform him that a visitor wished to see him.

"Who is he?"

"He gave no name, sir. He's part Indian but speaks perfect English."

"Perhaps he's one of the spies I sent to Florida to scout the activities of the British there. Send him in."

A tall light-skinned man wearing moccasins and torn buckskins entered. "I am William Weatherford, Red Eagle," he said.

Jackson's hawklike eyes gleamed in surprise.

"I come to give myself up," Weatherford added. "I can fight you no longer. My best warriors are dead. Do with me as you please. I am in your power."

"You are not," Jackson cried, "in my power! My orders were to have Red Eagle brought to me in chains. But you've come of your own will. What do you want of me?"

Weatherford held himself proudly erect. "I want nothing for myself. But the Creek women and children are starving. They are without food, not even an ear of corn."

Jackson sighed. "We'll find your survivors, feed them, and help them however we can." He stood up and offered his hand. "You're free to go, Weatherford, as you came."

The tall war chief gripped the general's hand, bowed slightly, and walked out the door.

For a minute or so Jackson stood with his lips pressed together. "I expected he'd be a bloodthirsty savage," he said quietly, "and he turns out to be a civilized man. Captain Reid, the Creek War is ended."

2
The British Invaders

In the days following the surrender of Red Eagle, General Jackson permitted most of the Tennessee Volunteers to return home. He warned them, however, to be ready for immediate action if the British Army invaded along the Southern Coast.

Late in the spring, Jackson's scouts in the Spanish territory of Florida reported that several British agents had arrived there. The British were arming the Indians and had been consulting with the Spanish commander at Pensacola.

In June, General Jackson met with the defeated Creek chieftains. He hoped that from these councils he could obtain a treaty of peace which would last forever. He wanted no more wars with these hard-fighting Indians.

While the peace meetings were under way he received startling news from Europe. The Duke of Wellington had defeated Napoleon Bonaparte and the British were no longer at war with France.

"This means that our British enemies now have a huge army which they can send against us," Jackson said to Captain Reid. "We must prepare to fight."

"Do you still believe they will attack us from the Gulf of Mexico?"

"More than ever now," the general replied. "Florida is under weak Spanish rule and would make an excellent base for them." He began pacing up and down the small headquarters room. "I need a good man to scout the Spanish forts around Pensacola. I'd like to send you, but you are needed here. What's your opinion of Captain Gordon?"

"John Gordon," Reid said, "is an excellent frontiersman. A clever man with sharp eyes. He would know what to look for."

Jackson nodded and reached for a quill pen. "Have Captain Gordon report to me. I shall write out a message for him to deliver to the Spanish commandant at Pensacola."

Late in July, Captain Gordon returned from his mission to Florida. He was tanned and bearded and was wearing dusty buckskins. "That Spanish commander," Gordon said, "Don Matteo Manrique, he took your message as an insult, sir."

"It was meant as an insult," Jackson answered grimly, "if he allows the British to use Florida as a base for an attack on the United States."

"British soldiers are already there," Gordon continued. "They're building a supply base at the mouth of Apalachicola River. A British marine captain has issued arms and uniforms to a company of hostile Creeks and is drilling them."

Jackson turned and glared fiercely at a wall map showing the coastline of the Gulf of Mexico. "I

17

calculate we'll have some warm work before winter sets in. They'll try to send a war fleet into Mobile for sure— to put soldiers ashore." He pointed to the bottom of the map. "See that boot-shaped spit of land there below Mobile. An abandoned fort—Fort Bowyer—commands the water passage into Mobile. We must reoccupy it and repair its guns before the British arrive, if we hope to keep their armies out of Mobile." His jaw thrust out angrily when he turned back to Captain Gordon. "The only force we have in reach is the Third Infantry. Five hundred men. But by the eternal, they'll do to keep the British out of Mobile."

On August 22, Jackson marched into Mobile with the Third Infantry Regiment. He immediately sent Major William Lawrence and one hundred and sixty men by boats to fortify Fort Bowyer. During the next few days alarming reports began arriving from his scouts in Florida. A British war fleet was gathering at Pensacola, only fifty miles from Fort Bowyer. More British troops had arrived, and their commander, Colonel Edward Nicholls, had issued a proclamation to the "natives of Louisiana" calling upon them to overthrow the American government. Colonel Nicholls promised that British soldiers and British-trained Indians would soon capture Mobile.

There were also rumors of another and larger British fleet massing in the West Indies. The fleet's purpose, so the rumors said, was to block the mouth of the Mississippi River. Then the British armies would invade Louisiana and capture New Orleans.

Not long afterward, even worse news reached General Jackson's headquarters. Far to the north, a British force had attacked Washington, burning the

Capitol and the White House. President James Madison and his Cabinet had fled the city. "It's a dark day for the United States," Jackson said when Captain Reid brought him the news. "But the British have not beaten us yet."

On September 14, the general boarded a schooner for a sail down Mobile Bay to inspect Fort Bowyer's defenses. Along the way he met a small boat. Aboard this vessel was a messenger from Major Lawrence. The British had landed a party of marines and Indians in the rear of Fort Bowyer.

Without delay, General Jackson ordered the schooner to turn about and head for Mobile at the fastest possible speed. Reinforcements would be needed for Major Lawrence. As soon as he reached Mobile, he was handed another message. His spies along the coast had sighted a British war fleet in full sail for Fort Bowyer.

3
The Battle of
Fort Bowyer

On the upper battlement of Fort Bowyer, Major William Lawrence lifted his spyglass and watched four British warships rounding the point. In another hour they would be in range of the fort's guns.

Immediately below him was a semicircular battery facing the narrow channel into Mobile Bay. Major Lawrence was hopeful that his guns could cripple any ship trying to sail past. Nor could a landing party overrun the fort from the beach below. Even if the British succeeded in storming the slope, they would be stopped by a twenty-foot moat filled with slimy water.

What worried Major Lawrence was the force of British marines and Indians that had landed in the rear of the fort. The narrow peninsula behind Fort Bowyer was overgrown with briers and live oaks; it was also broken by ditches and ravines. Half a mile to the southeast were sand dunes higher than the fort. If the enemy could place artillery there, a ground attack under a protective bombardment would probably follow.

After one more glance at the approaching warships,

Major Lawrence went down for a final inspection. Most of his one hundred and sixty officers and men were infantrymen, but he had given them gunnery drill for three weeks and he was pleased at how well they performed. They had repaired the rotting carriages of the 12- and 24-pounder cannons and had fastened the 4- and 9-pounders to the bastions. The most serious weakness was in the fort itself—a lack of casements to shelter his gunners. They would be exposed to enemy fire from above their knees. Major Lawrence was also concerned about the pine log parapets. The wood was dry and resinous and could easily be set afire by shell explosions.

A call from a sentry warned that the enemy's land force had been sighted on the dunes. "They're combining their attack with the approaching warships," Major Lawrence said. As he hurried toward the south side of the battery, an incoming shell screamed and exploded overhead. It was immediately followed by a 12-pounder ball which crashed into a timber supporting a parapet. Splinters flew through the air; a beam cracked and sagged.

The major ordered fire returned. His gunners swung another carriage into position, and two 12-pounders roared a reply. The British fired two more shells, but both exploded harmlessly in the air.

"They have at least two artillery pieces out there," Lawrence said. "A howitzer and a twelve-pounder." He also knew that he was outnumbered two to one and that a determined British officer, Colonel Edward Nicholls, was in personal command of the besieging force. Beyond the dunes a thin dust cloud arose and floated back out of range.

21

"They've pulled away, sir!" shouted an artillery officer.

"For the time being," Major Lawrence replied. His voice had a sharp edge to it. He turned back toward the shore side of the battery. The warships were trimming their sails as they turned into the channel.

Through his glass the major could read the name of the flagship which was in the lead—the *Hermes*. That would be Sir William H. Percy, commander of the fleet. Major Lawrence counted the carronades on the two larger ships. Twenty-four 32-pounders. The smaller brigs carried sixteen 24-pounders. Eighty guns against his twenty! And he was outmanned now by ten to one. The odds are impossible, Major Lawrence thought, and then he smiled grimly. He remembered Old Hickory Jackson saying that one free American could lick ten of the king's men any day of the week. At least, Major Lawrence promised himself, Colonel Nicholls and Commodore Percy will know they have been in a fight.

The *Hermes* was putting out its anchor now, and its sailors were launching several light boats. They rowed in toward the shoreline, stopping frequently to drop weighted lines over the sides of the boats. "They're taking soundings," Lawrence said, "to see if the water is deep enough to bring the warships in close and blast our walls apart. Let's give them a shower of grapeshot." Bursting shells sent the light boats scurrying back toward the *Hermes*. They returned again about dusk, but another shelling chased them away. After nightfall, Major Lawrence again heard the splash of oars and guessed the British warships would move in with the next day's tide.

At daybreak of September 15, Major Lawrence was

22

on the battlement again, watching as winds swept fog out into the Gulf of Mexico and cleared the skies. For two or three hours, signalmen on the British ships were busy exchanging messages with the marines ashore. Before noon the breeze slackened and the ships began lifting their anchors. With Commodore Percy's *Hermes* in the lead, they moved out into the Gulf, tacked their sails, and then bore down at full speed against the fort.

As soon as the warships were in reach of Fort Bowyer's guns, Major Lawrence accepted the challenge. He ordered his men to open fire from his two 24-pounders. In reply, the *Hermes* fired one of her forward guns, but the ball buried itself in the beach below. Major Lawrence then ordered all his guns along the channel side to open with brisk fire.

Commodore Percy now made it plain that he was determined to destroy or capture Fort Bowyer. In spite of the heavy firing, he brought the *Hermes* to anchor directly opposite the fort's circular battery, stationing his other three ships in line of battle down the channel. A few minutes later the four ships discharged whole broadsides. Shells shrieked and exploded; cannonballs pounded against wood and stone, shaking the fort. But Major Lawrence's gunners held steady, directing a savage bombardment upon the two nearest warships.

In the midst of this duel between fort and ships, the marines on the land side opened fire with their two big guns. During the night the British had emplaced these weapons behind a sand dune a few hundred yards from the fort. For several minutes, shot and shell raked Fort Bowyer's poorly protected south battery, inflicting the first casualties on the American defenders. Certain that the British marines and their Indian allies would come swarming in unless this barrage could be stopped, Major Lawrence ordered all movable guns turned against the sand dune. A concentration of canister and grapeshot brought quick results; the enemy's land guns ceased firing.

On the channel side, the duel now began raging with redoubled fury. Thick smoke swirled around both fort and ships. Then, through a sudden opening in the screen of smoke, Major Lawrence saw that the flag on the *Hermes* was no longer flying.

Uncertain as to whether the flag had been shot down or lowered as a sign of surrender, Lawrence ordered his men to hold their fire. For five minutes, not a gun was fired on either side. Just as the major was about to signal a demand for surrender, he heard commands echoing from the brig below the flagship. A full broadside flung a hail of metal against the battery wall.

Lawrence immediately shouted a command to return fire. During the five-minute lull every one of his guns had been reloaded, and for the first time in the engagement they were fired in unison. The resulting blast shook the flooring under his feet, and when the smoke cleared away, he saw the *Hermes* drifting helplessly toward the shore. Shot from the heavy bombardment had cut the flagship's anchor cable. As soon as the channel current pulled the ship's bow around to the fort, Lawrence's flashing guns raked the *Hermes'* decks fore and aft.

By this time the sun was setting and the British seamen were more than ready to call it a day. While the *Hermes* drifted into the shallows, the other three warships lifted anchors and moved out of range into the Gulf. Until darkness fell, the jubilant gunners inside

Fort Bowyer continued firing on the flagship. They also drove back a halfhearted land attack from the marines.

About nine o'clock that night a blaze suddenly appeared on the deck of the *Hermes*. Tongues of flame flared up into the sails and not long afterward reached the powder magazine. The explosion was a tremendous flash and roar sending billowing fireballs into the dark sky.

"We've beaten them!" Major Lawrence cried. "We've beaten the British!" The cheering inside Fort Bowyer was deafening.

At his headquarters in Mobile that same day, Andrew Jackson paced anxiously up and down, awaiting news from Fort Bowyer. During the night he ordered Captain William Laval to load a company of men on a boat and hurry down the bay to reinforce Fort Bowyer.

Early the next morning Captain Laval and his men returned. They had been unable to approach Fort Bowyer because of a fierce battle. The British were attacking the fort from both land and sea. After nightfall a great explosion had occurred, and Captain Laval feared that the fort's powder magazine had blown up. If this were true, the fort had surely surrendered, and the captain decided he should return to aid in the defense of Mobile.

General Jackson was dismayed by this news. He knew that Colonel Coffee was marching from Tennessee with several companies of Volunteers, but if the British had captured Fort Bowyer, the enemy could arrive before the Tennesseans. In that case, the general knew he must defend Mobile with what was left of the Third Infantry Regulars—less than four hundred men.

After several more anxious hours of waiting, news of Major Lawrence's victory finally arrived. Instead of the fort's powder magazine, it had been the British flagship that Captain Laval had seen blown up in the darkness. Both the sea and land forces of the enemy had gone limping back to the safety of their Florida base.

When the general's aide, Captain Reid, delivered this message, he was pleased to see a smile break across Old Hickory's solemn face. "The first thing we do now, John," the general said, "is to demand a promotion for Will Lawrence. He's a fighter and I like fighters. The second thing is to strike the British again—while they're still reeling from shock. John Coffee and the Volunteers should be here in a few days. This time we shan't wait for the British to come to us. This time we're going into Florida."

"Into Florida, sir? That's Spanish territory. Should we not have permission from the War Department in Washington?"

Andrew Jackson shut his jaw hard, then spoke firmly: "We don't know if the War Department has returned to Washington since the British invaded there. By the time we could hear from our War Department it would be too late. No, Captain Reid, I must act as if I were the government. I must succeed in this, of course. If I should fail in Florida, that would be the end of Major General Andrew Jackson."

4
Laffite the Pirate

About two hundred miles west of Andrew Jackson's Mobile headquarters, a British sloop of war was approaching the green island Grand Terre on the Louisiana coast. Captain Nicholas Lockyer stared at the yellow beach, and then beyond it he saw a small brick fort. No flag was flying above the rampart.

"Fire the signal gun!" Captain Lockyer ordered. A few minutes later he smiled with satisfaction at the sight of a boat putting out from shore with five men aboard. Lockyer turned to the man beside him. "Captain McWilliams," he said, "we'll lower my gig and row to meet them."

McWilliams wore the uniform of the Royal Colonial Marines. "I go well armed," he replied and pushed his black varnished hat tightly down on his head. "I don't trust Jean Laffite and his buccaneer crew."

Lockyer made a scoffing noise in his throat. "Laffite's Baratarian pirates respect the power of the British Navy," he said and stepped down toward the deck.

A hundred yards off shore, the captain's gig and the

pirates' boat met in gently rolling waves. "We wish to see Monsieur Jean Laffite," McWilliams shouted.

One of the boatmen replied in French: "You will find Laffite onshore."

A few minutes later the British sailors leaped into the surf and hauled the boat onto the beach. Lockyer and McWilliams stepped out on the damp sand and turned to face the Baratarians. The tallest of the five pirates was deeply tanned. His wavy brown hair was quite long. He was barefoot and wore a faded green shirt and baggy sailcloth trousers. "At your service, gentlemen," he said mockingly in French.

Meanwhile, more than a hundred Baratarians armed with knives and pistols were gathering on the beach. Captain McWilliams gave them a nervous glance and then said to the tall boatman: "I have a packet of letters for Jean Laffite."

"I will deliver them to Monsieur Laffite."

With some misgivings, Captain McWilliams withdrew a small canvas package from his coat pocket and handed it to the pirate, who took it with an exaggerated bow. "Follow me," he commanded and led the way toward the fort.

In front of the fort was a low-roofed porch with several hammocks swung from posts. The tall pirate motioned to the two British officers to wait there, and then he went on into the fort.

For several minutes McWilliams and Lockyer waited. The crowd of Baratarians had followed them up from the beach. They were laughing among themselves and making loud insulting comments. Captain Lockyer took out his handkerchief and mopped his brow. "How long

28

must we wait here, McWilliams?" he asked in a low voice.

"My orders instructed me to see Laffite in person if possible," the marine officer replied.

The door off the porch swung open and Lockyer looked up, his eyes widening at what he saw. The tall pirate had returned, but he was now wearing dress clothes and neatly polished boots. He smiled, closed one eye in a long wink, and said in perfect English: "You will be my guests for dinner, gentlemen. I am Jean Laffite."

The three men dined in a richly furnished room inside the fort. Laffite sat at the head of a long table, with three sheets of paper spread out beside his plate. "I have read the letters," he said. "I am quite interested in the one from your Colonel Edward Nicholls. He has promised me the rank of captain in the British Navy if I will put my ships under his command."

"Yes," replied Captain McWilliams. "He will guarantee fair value for your ships."

Laffite glanced at one of the other letters. "Colonel Nicholls expects to attack New Orleans soon?" he asked.

McWilliams nodded. "He is hopeful that Laffite's Baratarians will guide us through the many bayous and lakes that surround the city. We will need small well-armed ships such as yours."

"I do not like the threatening tone of Captain Percy's letter. Who is this Captain Percy?"

McWilliams put down his silver fork. "Captain Percy is senior officer in command of His Majesty's war fleet, a commodore. If his words seem prideful to you, that is only his manner."

Laffite showed his white teeth in a humorless smile. "I have noted that British military officers are somewhat overbearing and overconfident—especially toward Americans."

"Ah, the Americans. Our purpose is to liberate them from their wicked government. We know the government of Louisiana unjustly arrested Dominique You and your brother Pierre for piracy and locked them in a New Orleans jail. You will help us to free them, will you not, Monsieur Laffite?"

Laffite stared gravely at the marine captain, ignoring the question. "Commodore Percy promises fair value for use of my ships. How much does he consider fair value?"

McWilliams hesitated a moment and then replied: "What would you say to thirty thousand in gold?"

"The amount, sir, must be discussed with my partners. I cannot give you an answer before morning." Laffite pushed his chair back from the table and stood up.

The two British officers also rose. "Then we'll return to our ship," Captain Lockyer said. "Until tomorrow."

"I would prefer that you remain here, gentlemen," Laffite replied curtly. "My men have made your sailor escorts comfortable, and you will have the best of quarters."

Lockyer halted in midstride, surprised to see armed guards standing in each door of the dining room. "Show our guests to their quarters," Laffite ordered, and then he smiled at Lockyer's whispered words: "We're trapped in a den of pirates, McWilliams!"

During the next hour Jean Laffite sat at his desk, carefully writing two important letters. "I will never let

30

slip any occasion of serving my country, or of proving that she has never ceased to be dear to me," he began. "I hope this proof of loyalty to the United States of America will help the situation of my unhappy brothers, Pierre Laffite and Dominique You."

After he finished writing, he folded the letters around the ones that had been brought to him by the British officers. Then he fastened them securely in the canvas wrapper and called for a messenger. A swarthy young man wearing a gold ring in one ear appeared almost immediately.

"Jules, I want this package delivered to Jean Blanque in New Orleans," Laffite said. "Tell Monsieur Blanque to open it at once, that I wish him to deliver in person the letter I have written to Governor Claiborne."

The swarthy young man, Jules Ranchier, blinked his eyes in surprise. "You have written a letter to the governor of Louisiana?"

"That is no affair of yours, Jules," Laffite replied bluntly. "You will wait for the governor's reply and bring it back to me at once. *Allez au trot!* Go quickly!"

Next morning during a leisurely breakfast with his two nervous guests Jean Laffite informed them that he would have to wait several days before giving them a reply. "I must consult with others who are not here at the fort," Laffite explained.

"Your brother Pierre, perhaps," McWilliams guessed. "He is in irons in a New Orleans jail. Why must you delay, sir? Join with us, and we'll free your brother in a matter of weeks. We'll also make you a rich man."

Laffite shook his head. "Gentlemen, it is impossible for me to say yes or no at this time. Come back in two weeks and I will give you my answer."

31

He walked with them to the beach where their sailors and the gig waited. For some minutes Laffite stood there, watching them row out to the warship.

A few days later, Jules Ranchier returned from New Orleans. "Have you no letter for me, Jules?" Laffite demanded.

"No letter, Jean."

Laffite's tanned face turned dark with anger. "Does Governor Claiborne have nothing to say to me, then?"

"Monsieur Blanque said to tell you that the governor desires you to make no bargain with the British until you hear from him. The governor promises in the meantime to forgive you for smuggling goods into New Orleans, but he cannot make any promises concerning pardons for Pierre and Dominique."

Laffite laughed. "Governor Claiborne is a *vieille femme,* a timid old lady. Very well, but we shall give him time."

For several more days, Jean Laffite waited impatiently, but he heard nothing further from the governor of Louisiana. Promptly on the fourteenth day following the visit of the British officers, a warship appeared again off Grand Terre Island. For a day or so the vessel drifted about the coast. With amused contempt, Jean Laffite watched the British ship, but he made no move to send a boat out with his reply.

"I am betting on Governor Claiborne's fear of the British to bring him around to pardoning Pierre and Dominique," he said to Jules Ranchier. "Claiborne wants my Baratarians on his side when the British attack New Orleans. My guess is the governor is waiting to get an opinion from Old Hickory, General Andrew Jackson."

5
Long March to Florida

A few days later in Mobile, Captain John Reid knocked on General Jackson's door. "Come in," the general called out, and Captain Reid said: "A messenger from Governor Claiborne of Louisiana, sir."

"From Claiborne? Bring the messenger in, John. Let's hope the governor is sending us the Louisiana Volunteers I asked for."

The messenger dropped a saddlebag on the floor and saluted briskly. "Lieutenant Mercier of the Orleans Dragoons reporting, sir, for Governor Claiborne."

"Be at your ease, Lieutenant. Sit there on that bench beside Captain Reid." The general smiled at the self-conscious movements of the red-faced young militia officer. "What news do you bring from Governor Claiborne?"

The lieutenant sprang forward to the saddlebag, fumbled at the straps, and brought forth a canvas packet. "Messages, sir. The governor discussed the contents with me should the general desire more details."

"Excellent," Jackson said and emptied the packet on

33

his desk. He propped his booted legs on an empty chair and began scanning the letters. He grunted, cleared his throat, clicked his tongue, and then frowned severely at Lieutenant Mercier. "Confound it, Lieutenant, the governor has written not one word in reply to my request for Louisiana troops. All he seems concerned with are bandits, the Laffite brothers. Surely Governor Claiborne does not believe these British papers are genuine?"

Lieutenant Mercier tugged nervously at his collar. "The governor is certain the British are preparing to attack New Orleans."

"So he asks me to bring my soldiers to New Orleans instead of sending Louisiana soldiers to me." The general dropped his feet to the floor with a loud indignant thump. "These letters must be forgeries, a trick of Jean Laffite to get his pirate brothers free from jail."

"Pierre Laffite is already free, sir. He escaped just before I left New Orleans."

"No! By thunder, no man could break out of the New Orleans calaboose without help from outside. Pierre Laffite's escape must have been arranged."

"That is a rumor, I believe. But Governor Claiborne has offered a reward for his recapture."

"Pettifoggery!" Jackson roared. "I have no taste for dealing with pirates and smugglers. Captain Reid, will you take a look at these British letters?"

For several minutes, Reid examined the messages. "I have no way of knowing whether the signatures are genuine, sir, but the paper they are written on seems to be British military stationery. I'm sure I can find matching sheets among the messages our spies captured in Florida."

34

"No need." Jackson raised his hand. "It could still be a clever British trick to draw us off in the wrong direction. But I must admit the statement about a large British fleet 'pushing for New Orleans' disturbs me. All the more reason we should strike their Florida base at once. Then we can turn our attention to defending New Orleans." He sighed. "Show Lieutenant Mercier to quarters. I shall write a reply to Governor Claiborne this evening."

During the next few days, General Jackson was too busy assembling his army of invasion to give much thought to the Laffite letters. From Tennessee, Colonel John Coffee arrived with almost two thousand Volunteers. "Every one of my boys," Coffee declared, "wants to get within fair buck range of a Redcoat."

"They'll have their chance very soon, Colonel Coffee, very soon," Jackson promised him.

A regiment of dragoons and a company of friendly Choctaw also marched in from Mississippi. From forts above Mobile came units of the Thirty-ninth and Forty-fourth Regulars to join the Third Infantry.

On November 2, Andrew Jackson started his invasion column marching up the valley of the Mobile River—three thousand men inspired with Old Hickory's determination to drive the British from their bases on Pensacola Bay. By direct line across the coast the distance was only 60 miles, but the marshlands were impassable. Jackson therefore led his column northward to Fort Stoddard, swung eastward to Fort Montgomery, and then turned south. The long route was more than 100 miles, but at the end of four days marching, Jackson halted the forward company of the Forty-fourth Infantry on the outskirts of Pensacola.

With Major Henry Peire of the Forty-fourth, Jackson rode down the sandy trail for a closer look at the nearest fort, St. Michael. Beyond the bristling guns of the fort were seven British men-of-war in the bay.

"We'll camp out of range of their guns," Jackson said. He glanced at the sun. "We have at least three hours of daylight left, Major Peire. I'm sending you with a truce party to Fort St. Michael. We'll give the Spanish commandant a chance to avoid bloodshed. My terms are the surrender of forts St. Michael and Barrancas and the battery on Santa Rosa. To be garrisoned by United States soldiers until Spain drives the British from Florida."

"Do you believe the Spaniard will agree to that, sir?" Major Peire asked respectfully.

"At least we'll give him a choice." Jackson wheeled his horse. "The Mississippi Dragoons are coming in from reconnaissance patrol. I'll order a platoon forward to escort you. My aide, Captain Reid, will supply you with a truce flag."

A few minutes later Major Peire and his escort, with a large white banner flapping in the breeze, rode down the trail toward Fort St. Michael. General Jackson dismounted and walked over to an oak tree where Captain Reid was resting. "We'll know soon, John, whether or not we must fight them," he said quietly.

Fifteen minutes later, they had the answer: a booming explosion from one of Fort St. Michael's 12-pounders. The dragoons and Major Peire came galloping back, the truce flag dragging over the rump of the bearer's horse.

Jackson strode out into the road, his boots sinking in the loose sand. The long tails of his unbuttoned coat

36

swirled in a gust of wind off the bay. "They fired on your truce flag, Major?" he shouted.

"In defiance of the laws of nations, they fired upon us, sir!" Major Peire was breathing hard. "We saw Redcoats up there, General. British uniforms on the redoubts."

Jackson turned slowly, shading his eyes against the setting sun. "Prepare yourself to spend a busy night, Captain Reid. At dawn tomorrow, we'll storm Pensacola!"

6
The Battle of Pensacola

It was a busy night for all of Andrew Jackson's staff officers. They gathered in the general's tent, where Captain John Gordon and members of the spy company gave them detailed descriptions of Pensacola. Captain Gordon answered questions about the forts, locations of cannon in the town, condition of the roads, streets and beaches.

During the meeting Jackson sat near a fluttering candle, sketching a crude map on a sheet of paper. "We'll attack in three columns," he announced at the end of the conference. "The Spaniards built their defenses for attacks from the west, so it will be Colonel Coffee's task to make them *believe* we are so foolish as to come in from the west. Your Tennesseans will make a noisy demonstration, Colonel Coffee, but warn your officers to keep their men out of range of the guns of Fort St. Michael. While Colonel Coffee is pretending to attack, Major Blue and his Volunteers will encircle the town along the narrow beach on the east. At the same time Major Woodruff will lead the Regulars in a center attack right into the streets of Pensacola. We move before daylight. See to your troops, gentlemen."

An hour before sunrise on November 7, Jackson's army was on the march. Every man was under strict orders to move silently. Jackson rode with the Regulars, just behind their artillery pieces, which rolled noiselessly in the sand. He was dressed in his best uniform, with golden epaulets on his shoulders and a new plume in his shako headpiece. To keep out the chill of the autumn morning he wrapped a gray woolen scarf around his neck.

As first dawn light streaked the sky across the bay, volleys of musket fire crackled from the west. "John Coffee is kindling the blaze," Jackson said. "Can't we move these caissons a bit faster, Major Woodruff?"

"Sand is dragging at the wheels, sir. I'll put some men to heave at the spokes."

Jackson urged his horse into a faster gait. "I'm going forward," he shouted back to Captain Reid. As he hurried along the side of the marching regiment he could hear Coffee's Volunteers keeping up a steady firing.

Ahead in the gray light were dim shapes of rooftops and garden walls. Lanterns flickered palely in the streets. The advance company came to a halt as he overtook the rear squad. Captain William Laval came dashing back on his horse. "General Jackson," he acknowledged with surprise. "How far back is our artillery?"

"Half a mile at least. Bogged in sand. What're the Spaniards doing?"

"They're wide awake, sir. My scouts report a battery

unlimbered at the head of the street. Spanish infantrymen are forming behind walls."

Jackson squinted at the rim of sun coming over the horizon and then stared at the town. Shadowy figures darted from house to house.

"We'll not wait for the artillery, Captain. Attack now before they're ready for us."

"Right, sir!" Laval turned his horse around and hurried to the head of the column. As he dismounted he tossed the reins to a soldier, who quickly led the horse off the road.

Jackson sat calmly in his saddle, watching Laval form his company into a skirmish line. In a few moments they were charging into Pensacola. Small-arms fire rattled from a long wall to the left. Laval's infantrymen swarmed over and around it, silencing the Spanish marksmen. Then from the street came the blast of a cannon, showering shot. Some of it pattered on the leaves of the trees where General Jackson waited. Almost immediately he heard Captain Laval's shrill command: "Charge the battery!" Another cannon burst shook the ground.

Major Woodruff had arrived now, and Jackson ordered him to send companies to left and right to clear sharpshooters from roofs and walls. One more blast sounded from the cannon, and then a loud roar of cheering brought a quick smile to Jackson's lips. He spurred his horse forward and galloped into the town.

With pointed bayonets, a squad of American infantrymen was herding a group of Spanish prisoners down a side street. Along the sidewalk near the cannon, several Americans lay wounded. Recognizing Captain Laval among them, Jackson dismounted and hurried over to him. A sergeant was kneeling beside the captain. The yellow collar of Laval's dark-green blouse was stained with blood.

"How bad is it, Sergeant?" the general asked.

"Flesh wound, sir. I've sent for the surgeon."

Laval's eyelids fluttered, then opened wide when he saw Andrew Jackson peering anxiously down at him. "We captured their battery, General. How is the fighting going?"

"I think the Spaniards have quit on us, Captain. And you've won yourself a major's rank."

A voice cut in: "General Jackson, sir."

"Yes?"

"A Spanish official wishes to see the general. He's in the next street bearing a truce flag."

A few moments later, General Jackson stood face to face with a white-haired stoop-shouldered gentleman whose trembling hands revealed his fear. "I, sir, am Don Matteo Gonzalez Manrique, commandant of Pensacola. Permit me to offer my respects to Señor Don Andres Jackson."

"No respects necessary," Jackson replied gruffly. "Where are your friends, the British?"

Manrique threw up his hands. "Fled to Fort Barrancas at the mouth of the bay. Our friends, as you call them, have proved untrustworthy."

Jackson grunted. A dozen Americans lie wounded and dying back in the street, he thought, because of this man's dealings with enemies of the United States. But he held back a flow of angry words and spoke softly: "Perhaps you have learned a lesson, Commandant Manrique. Are you ready to talk terms with me, as representative of the United States?"

41

Manrique bowed. "I invite you, sir, to be my guest at Government House."

Jackson turned and saw Captain Reid waiting expectantly behind him. "Bring along an infantry escort, Captain."

At the entrance to Pensacola's Government House, two uniformed guards stared uneasily at the American soldiers accompanying their commander, but Manrique waved them aside. Captain Reid posted American guards beside the Spaniards and followed the general and the commandant inside.

Manrique's reception room was small but richly furnished. Mementos of Spain covered the walls and tables. "The morning is chilly," the commandant said politely. "Would you care for brandy, señors?"

Jackson shook his head, his gaze shifting with amusement from one object in the room to another. "Let us come quickly to the point, Commandant. Our terms are simple. We ask the Spanish government to agree that Pensacola, St. Michael and Barrancas shall be occupied by American troops."

Manrique smiled. "You must first drive the British troops from Barrancas in order to occupy it."

"That is my concern," Jackson retorted. "Do you accept the terms?"

"For how long, señor?"

"Until we have driven the British from America."

The Spaniard's fingers tapped nervously on his chair arm. "That will be a long time perhaps."

"Do you accept the terms?" Jackson repeated harshly.

The commandant's white-maned head dipped forward. "I understand now why your men call you Old

Hickory. I shall dispatch a messenger to Colonel Sotto, commander of St. Michael, advising him to yield the fort to your soldiers."

Jackson rose from his chair, adjusting his sword as he did so. "While you are awaiting a reply from Colonel Sotto, I have duties to perform. I shall return within an hour."

As the day wore on, Andrew Jackson's hot temper was more than once brought to the boiling point. It was first directed at the British ships which remained insolently at anchor in the bay. The British gunners occasionally sent rock-fire shells shrieking into the shoreline. Jackson had no way of getting at the ships, and he knew that Commodore Percy was letting him know that his fire shells could set the town ablaze whenever he chose to lift the elevation of his guns.

Jackson was hopeful that he could bottle the war fleet up in the bay if he could seize Fort Barrancas, but he knew that he dared not risk an attack on Barrancas without first occupying St. Michael. To his disgust, he had to wait until noon before a reply came from the commander of St. Michael.

In flowery language, Colonel Sotto replied that he could not obey his commandant's orders because his commandant was a prisoner of the Americans. The colonel added that he would not dishonor the Spanish flag by lowering it in surrender.

Jackson's temper exploded. "We'll give this Colonel Sotto half an hour to change his mind!" he shouted. He immediately ordered Captain James Dinkins of the Forty-fourth Infantry to take two companies of infantry and three artillery pieces within range of Fort St.

Michael. "Captain Dinkins, you will approach the fort under a truce flag. Tell the Spaniards we have no time to waste here, and that you are under my orders to take possession of the fort. As soon as you have a reply, send it by messenger to me."

As Dinkins marched off with his artillery, a courier arrived from Major Uriah Blue on the beach. The major reported that British soldiers were being lowered in boats from the sides of the ships. "If the Redcoats are not bluffing us," the general growled, "they're fools! John Coffee's sharpshooters can pick them off before their keels scrape the sand." He ordered five hundred Volunteers to march double time to reinforce Major Blue's companies. Then with a sigh of impatience, he turned to Major Peire. "We should have had a column on the march for Barrancas hours ago," he said. "Major Peire, I'm placing you in command of Pensacola. Captain Reid and I will round up the reserves and what men are not needed here and ready them for the march to Barrancas. We'll need Captain Dinkins' guns, of course. Inform me at once if there is any delay."

By late afternoon the Barrancas column was ready to march. Jackson was striding up and down the sandy road when a courier came galloping out from Pensacola. The general read the message hurriedly and handed it to Captain Reid. "Colonel Sotto refuses to see Captain Dinkins!" he cried. "The colonel accepts our conditions but says he can't surrender before morning. What manner of fools does he think we are, Captain?" Jackson's face was dark with anger. "The Spaniards are stalling for time. They're either expecting the British to come back and help them, or they're giving the British time to sail their ships past Barrancas and safely out of the bay!"

Not until Andrew Jackson marched most of his three thousand men into view of the fort, and threatened to attack in force, did Colonel Sotto realize the game was ended. Late in the evening, the colonel marched his troops out in smart formation and surrendered his sword. Jackson promptly ordered the weapon returned and began preparing for an early morning march down the coast to capture Fort Barrancas.

Next morning, to Jackson's dismay, he discovered that the British fleet off Pensacola had vanished. "I fear they've escaped," he said gloomily. "But we'll march for Barrancas. With that fort in our hands we can keep them from returning to Pensacola."

This time, however, the British outguessed Andrew Jackson. During the afternoon, the Americans' forward scouts heard a tremendous explosion. Soon afterward they could see smoke lifting high in the gray November sky. The British had blown up the fortifications and their war fleet had put out to sea.

Where was the British fleet bound for? Jackson puzzled over the question. Back to the West Indies to unite with a larger fleet rumored to be there? To Mobile? Or to New Orleans? He shook his head doubtfully and then made up his mind what he must do. He would leave enough men to garrison Pensacola and then return by forced march to Mobile. "If there's no sign of the enemy around Mobile," he said, "perhaps we'd better attend to those letters from Laffite and his pirates. New Orleans may be the place, after all."

7
New Orleans Welcomes Old Hickory

Ten days later, Andrew Jackson was holding a council of war at his headquarters in Mobile. "If I were the British commander in chief—and heaven forbid me that so-called honor—I would land my forces somewhere around Mobile," he said to his officers. "Then I would cut across the undefended open country north of New Orleans, seal that city off from the United States, and capture it when I pleased."

He picked up a bundle of messages from his desk and spread them out. "All the information we can gather, however, points to a British invasion directly from the Gulf of Mexico upon New Orleans. Many of these rumors are public knowledge in that city, and the people are begging for soldiers to defend them. I have a report here from a trusted friend in New Orleans. He fears that some of the merchants who have grown rich from trading with the British may try to make a deal with them and surrender the city. Therefore, I've decided to move my headquarters to New Orleans."

The general swung around in his chair to examine the map sketched on the wall planking. "We cannot leave

Mobile undefended. Most of the Regulars will stay here and at Fort Bowyer. At least a thousand mounted Volunteers will be needed to patrol the Gulf coast. Colonel Coffee and the remainder of the Volunteers will march overland to Baton Rouge to guard the western approaches. This leaves me very few troops to take to New Orleans, but I have the promise of two more regiments from Tennessee and Kentucky by Christmas. I hope to find several hundred militiamen in New Orleans. My informants tell me the best fighters are Laffite's Baratarian smugglers, but I do not intend to enlist bandits into my army."

On the morning of December 2, Andrew Jackson rode into the outskirts of New Orleans. He was accompanied by Captain Reid and a few officers and men of the Seventh Regular Infantry. After ten days on horseback he looked thin and gaunt. His hair had not been cut for weeks, and iron-gray ringlets sprouted from the edges of his tight leather cap. His blue cloak, tight pants, and dragoon boots were spattered with dried mud. As he approached a small welcoming party in carriages, his keen ears overheard a half-whispered remark: "He looks like an ugly old Kentucky flatboatman." Jackson's lips loosened in a slight smile, and then he dismounted to shake hands with Governor William Claiborne.

Transferring to the governor's carriage, the general rode on into the city. Rain began to fall, but waiting crowds along the streets remained to greet him with cheers: "Old Hickory! Old Hickory!" He waved his leather cap to them.

At the Place d'Armes (a New Orleans square which would later be named for him) General Jackson was delighted to find four companies of militia waiting in the downpour. He passed along the smartly formed lines, stopping often to inspect a weapon. His quick eye told him that at least half the muskets had no flints in the locks, but he decided to say nothing of this until later. Now was not the time to find fault with these green militiamen whose rain-streaked faces showed how pleased they were to see him.

That afternoon he opened headquarters at Number 106 Royal Street. Among his first visitors were two officers of the U.S. Navy, Commander Daniel Patterson and Lieutenant Thomas Catesby Jones. Their spotless uniforms contrasted sharply with the general's travel-stained cloak and trousers. "Accept my apologies, gentlemen, for the condition of my uniform," he said, "but I have been too busy to change."

"We are honored and relieved, General Jackson," the commander replied, "that you have come to New Orleans. I pledge full cooperation from the Navy." He introduced Lieutenant Jones.

"Can the Navy lend the Army any arms and ammunition?" Jackson asked bluntly.

Commander Patterson's ruddy face turned solemn. "Small arms are in short supply, I regret to say. Our last shipment of goods brought us gunpowder but no rifles or flints."

"Flints!" Jackson shouted, then quickly lowered his voice. "I have a report from the governor that there are only twenty-five hundred muskets in the entire city. And half of them useless for want of flints. We must scour New Orleans for flints, Commander Patterson." His hawk eyes softened for a moment. "I've also been studying the governor's maps. How many vessels do you have in service here, Commander?"

"Two warships, the *Louisiana* and the *Carolina*. Each carrying fifteen guns. Five gunboats armed with five guns each. A tender, the *Seahorse*. A dispatch boat. And my gig, which we call the *Alligator*."

"Can you put the gunboats into Lake Borgne by tomorrow?"

Patterson glanced at Lieutenant Jones. "They will be under your command, Lieutenant."

"The gunboats can be under sail this evening, sir," Jones promised.

"Good." The general nodded at the alert lieutenant. "If the British attack New Orleans, they probably will come into Lake Borgne from the Gulf. Keep a sharp eye on the islands at the entrance. Especially Ship Island and Cat Island. Report anything you see."

Commander Patterson spoke up: "Most of my seamen will be needed to man the gunboats, General. The *Louisiana* and *Carolina* will be left without sufficient crews or gunners."

"New Orleans is a port, Commander Patterson. Recruit more sailors."

The commander shook his head. "The only seasoned recruits would be Laffite's Baratarians. They are skilled cannoneers, but—"

"They're pirates!" Jackson finished the statement. "No, Commander, if events make it necessary, Lieutenant Jones can transfer his seamen back to your ships. We'll try to fight the British without using bandits."

Early the following day Andrew Jackson set out on a

tour of the country around New Orleans. By carriage, on horseback, and aboard boats he examined roads, streams, and sluggish bayous. Before nightfall he ordered out detachments of soldiers to cut trees across trails and waterways leading into the city from south, east, and west. He reinforced fortifications along the Mississippi River and set up new artillery positions at strategic points.

That evening when he returned to headquarters, two messages were waiting for him. One was from Lieutenant Jones on Lake Borgne. The naval officer's roving gunboats had sighted British vessels off Ship Island, about thirty small sloops of war. "Not surprising," Jackson said to Captain Reid. "But it may be a British trick. Drawing our attention to that place when they mean to strike at another. We'll watch them there—but be ready to meet them from whatever direction they come."

He reached for the other message, his eyes widening when he recognized the signature: Jean Laffite. "The smuggler insists he can help me," Jackson commented as he read the letter. "If I will free his fellow pirate, Dominique You, from jail, I will have Napoleon Bonaparte's best artillerist. So Laffite says, and adds that he will come to see me if I will send him a safe-conduct pass." Jackson brushed back a strand of hair that had fallen over his forehead. "No, Captain Reid, we need every man and gun we can scrape out of Louisiana, but I will not deal with outlaws in jail or in hiding."

8
The Battle of Lake Borgne

On December 12 aboard U.S. Gunboat Number 156, Lieutenant Thomas Catesby Jones led his small flotilla through Pass Christian and along the north edge of Cat Island. As his boat cleared the east peninsula he gasped in astonishment at what he saw in the blue waters of the sound. Only three days earlier he had counted thirty British ships in those same waters. Now there was twice that number—an array of gun brigs and cutters, a line of barges fitted with long oars, and farther out, several large warships.

Lieutenant Jones wasted no time in turning about. As soon as he sighted his dispatch boat off Point Claire, he put a signalman to work passing on his estimate of the increased British strength. For the remainder of the day he played a game of hide-and-seek with the British on Lake Borgne. His mission was to serve as Old Hickory's eyes, to report what the British were doing, what direction they might take. If challenged, Jones was to retreat across Lake Borgne to the entrance of Lake Pontchartrain. "There, with the help of our land guns,"

Commander Patterson had told him, "you will sink the enemy or be sunk!"

Next morning, Lieutenant Jones set his sails for Bay St. Louis. About four o'clock in the afternoon he sighted several British barges set low in the water, heading west toward Pass Christian. Leaving his supply boat, the *Seahorse,* in Bay St. Louis, Jones changed his game to cat and mouse and tried to lure the barges toward Lake Pontchartrain and the land guns. But the wind died away at sundown, and a strong outgoing tide forced the gunboats to drop anchors about midnight.

At daybreak on December 14, Lieutenant Jones turned his spyglass eastward. More British barges had approached during the night. He counted forty-five of them in a line front. Their small flags drooped in the windless morning, but he could see the flash of oars. They were coming in for an attack in V-formation. The British officer in the bow of the lead boat was Captain Nicholas Lockyer, who several weeks earlier had visited Jean Laffite on Grand Terre Island.

Jones signaled Gunboat Number 25 to open fire on the enemy. Its guns thundered loudly, but the spinning balls splashed short. At the same time Jones noticed that four barges were turning leftward. In a moment he saw what they were after. His smallest boat, the *Alligator,* had fallen far behind. Jones quickly brought his gunboat into firing position, but the range was too great. The eight-man crew of the *Alligator* tried desperately to break away. They scored several hits with their single 4-pounder, but the British boats surrounded the *Alligator* and soon captured it.

Abandoning all hope of a breeze to fill his sails, Jones now prepared to "sink the enemy or be sunk" where he

52

was. He maneuvered his boat, Number 156, about two hundred yards nearer the enemy than his other four vessels. He anchored at center and ordered decks cleared for action. As soon as the barges came in range, his gunners opened a bombardment.

For a few minutes the British flotilla gave way under the barrage. Several barges fell out of formation, and their crewmen leaped or were flung into the lake. But Captain Lockyer ordered his boats to separate into three groups, and they were soon pushing forward again. He led fifteen of them directly into the fire of Number 156, taking a severe wound. At the same time the other two British sections were encircling the gunboats to right and left.

Each barge carried a short-nosed carronade in its bow, and these guns began pouring shot into the American boats. Lieutenant Jones was hit in the shoulder, but for another hour he refused to surrender. He knew that he could expect no help. He knew that his five gunboats and 182 men faced desperate odds against 45 barges and 1,200 men. Yet even after the barges closed in with grappling hooks, and British seamen boarded the gunboats, Lieutenant Jones and his men fought across the slippery decks with bayonets, pikes, and cutlasses. Then, about noon on that bleak December day, Lieutenant Jones surrendered, and the Battle of Lake Borgne was ended.

Across the lake in Bay St. Louis, the men aboard Jones' last surviving vessel, the *Seahorse,* had watched helplessly during the battle. They were trapped in the harbor by three British barges. Realizing his situation was hopeless, Sailing Master Johnson, in command of the *Seahorse,* ordered the boat set afire. A few minutes later he and his crew were hurrying across the marshlands, bound for New Orleans with the bad news.

On the morning of December 15, General Jackson was inspecting artillery emplacements east of New Orleans when a courier from headquarters brought him the news of the Battle of Lake Borgne. Jackson immediately mounted his horse and set out at a gallop for Royal Street.

Commander Patterson, his face grave with anxiety, was waiting for him in the headquarters reception room. "New Orleans is near to panic," Patterson said.

Exhausted from his hard ride, Jackson dropped on a sofa. He removed his muddy boots and sank back with a sigh. "We have lost our 'eyes' on Lake Borgne and you have lost some of your best seamen."

"I shall make a desperate try," Patterson replied firmly, "to recruit more men for my two warships."

Captain Reid brought in a message and handed it to the general. Jackson scanned it, then read it aloud to Commander Patterson: "Estimate ten thousand British soldiers on way by sea and land."

Patterson nodded. "Lieutenant Jones' last report came close to that number."

"We have only three thousand men," Jackson said. "And half of them with no arms fit for fighting."

"What do you propose to do, General?"

Jackson brought himself upright, bracing his hands on his bony knees. "I propose, Commander Patterson, to make New Orleans into an armed camp!"

"Will the people support you? In the coffeehouses there is already talk of abandoning the city."

The general's face turned scornful. "Cowards always

54

think first of running. I shall proclaim martial law. Every citizen must give his time and labor in preparation to meet the invading foe. No persons will be permitted to leave the city. No boats shall move from the wharves. The British will surely send in spies, therefore streetlamps will be extinguished at nine o'clock each night. After that time all persons found on the streets will be arrested as spies."

For the remainder of the day, General Jackson kept his staff busy writing and dispatching urgent messages. He sent orders to every outpost: "Defend your position as long as a man remains alive to point a gun." He sent messengers on fast horses to Colonel Coffee at Baton Rouge, ordering him to march his Volunteers immediately to New Orleans. He sent messengers on relays of horses to find Colonel William Carroll's Tennessee Volunteers who were coming down the river by flatboat. He sent out dozens of other couriers—up the Natchez Trace in search of General John Thomas' Kentuckians and to Mississippi for Colonel Thomas Hinds' Dragoons.

As the day ended, he leaned back on his sofa, wondering how long it would take the British to move their army and supplies within striking distance of New Orleans. Not more than a week, he guessed.

Outside his window came the sound of voices singing. They were singing "Yankee Doodle"! As the sound died away, another group started up the "Marseillaise" in French. Soon they were all shouting "Old Hickory! Old Hickory!"

So the people of New Orleans, French-speaking as well as English-speaking, did have confidence in him after all. They believed he could keep the British Army from taking their city. He arose and began pacing the room, his face grim with worry. To defeat ten thousand of the enemy, he must have more arms *and more men who knew how to fight!* Where could he find them?

9
Laffite the Patriot

An orderly was bringing lighted candles into the general's room when angry commands sounded suddenly from Royal Street. "See what that commotion is about," Jackson said.

A moment later, Captain Reid appeared at the door quite excited. "Sir, the lieutenant of the guard reports he has captured Jean Laffite. Laffite and two of his men were attempting to enter headquarters."

"Are you certain the man is Laffite?"

"He admits to being the genuine article and insists upon seeing the general. Shall we march him off to jail?"

Jackson turned his head to one side, pursing his lips in an odd smile. "If the man was willing to risk arrest to see me, I will hear what he has to say. We can jail him later."

After a short delay, Jean Laffite strode confidently into the room. He swept off his fur hat, bowed, and said: "It is not an easy matter for a simple man to see Old Hickory, but I assure you, sir, that the honor of doing so is worth all the difficulties." In his black coat and trousers, spotless white shirt, and flowing black tie, Laffite looked like a respectable businessman.

"You Frenchmen make pretty speeches," Jackson replied coldly. He remained standing and did not offer a chair to the Baratarian. "Speak to the point, man."

"Your pardon, sir. First, it is necessary that I make known to you my two companions who were not permitted to enter with me."

"Captain Reid!" Jackson thundered. "Send the other two men in!"

Laffite's companions were a strange pair. One was as neatly dressed as Laffite; he had long sideburns and his clipped hair came to a sharp point in the center of his forehead. The other man had a hooknose and a swarthy scarred face. He wore a seaman's jacket and breeches, and carried a duffle bag over one shoulder.

Laffite introduced the man with the pointed hairline as Captain Renato Beluche, adding that Beluche had been fighting his own private war with the British at sea for two years.

Piracy would be a better word for it, Jackson said to himself. Laffite then introduced the man with the hooknose as Alexandre Laffite. "My brother," Laffite continued, "but better known by the name of Dominique You."

General Jackson's bushy eyebrows raised slightly. "Dominique You is supposed to be in irons in the calaboose."

"The judge released him today," Jean Laffite explained calmly.

The general tried to conceal his surprise. "I suppose I need not ask why."

Dominique You was grinning broadly. "I told the

58

judge I could not fight the British in jail," he said with a heavy French accent.

"Well, what do you want of me?"

"We ask the honor of serving under your banners," Jean Laffite replied. "To prove that no one is more ready than we to defend the United States of America. It is our country as well as yours."

General Jackson clasped his hands behind his back and glared fiercely at his three visitors. "You have broken your country's laws."

"The laws we broke are unjust. They benefit rich men here in New Orleans who grow richer from trading with our enemies. Was not this country founded by the overthrow of unjust laws?"

"We wanted only to change the laws," Jackson declared. "To change them, not break them before changing."

Laffite shrugged. "Perhaps you are right. If we have done wrong against our country, that is all the more reason we should risk our lives for our country now." He added quickly: "It is known that you have only three thousand men, only a thousand trained Regulars. We can bring you a thousand Baratarians who have tasted fire and steel many times."

Laffite reached for the duffle bag on Dominique You's shoulder and drew out a rolled map. "Let me show you why you need us, Old Hickory." He flattened the map out on the desk. When General Jackson held a candle closer, he saw at once that Laffite's map was better than the one he had been using. Every swamp and bayou, every bay and inlet, was carefully marked. "My men know this watery country better than your militiamen know the streets of New Orleans," Laffite

59

said. He turned and looked squarely into the general's steel-blue eyes. "That is why the British wanted us to join with them. They had the sense to know they needed us."

Andrew Jackson held his temper. He did not like Laffite's easy insolence, but he admired men who spoke their minds.

"In these swamps we have cannon and ammunition hidden away so that only we can find them," Laffite continued. "We have dozens of the best cannoneers to fire them. Renato and Dominique can raise two companies of artillery in a matter of hours. Out there on the river you have two warships without crews or gunners. We can man them tomorrow."

Jackson's head rocked back so that he seemed to be staring at the ceiling. "You speak with persuasion, Jean Laffite," he said quietly.

"One other thing." Laffite reached into the duffle bag and drew out a handful of flints. "It is rumored that half your muskets have no flints. I can supply you with more than five thousand."

"Where did you find them?" Jackson demanded angrily. "My men turned New Orleans upside down searching for flints and found scarcely a dozen."

Laffite's white teeth flashed in a smile. "We captured them from a British ship, General."

For several seconds, Andrew Jackson's deep-set eyes remained fixed on the face of the smiling Baratarian. Then he broke into a roar of laughter. Laffite joined in, and then Beluche began chuckling, and soon Dominique You's hoarse guffaw was added to the chorus.

The door to the outer room opened suddenly, and

60

Captain Reid's puzzled face appeared. As the laughter died away, Jackson called to him: "I seem to have misjudged these bandits, Captain Reid. It would be foolish to persist in my mistaken notions. See that an order is issued to stop the reward offer for Mr. Pierre Laffite, and issue safe-conduct passes for Mr. Jean Laffite and his two companions."

Within a few hours, the promises made by Jean Laffite began to take shape. From Grand Terre Island and other islands along the coast, the Baratarians poured into New Orleans. They wore bright-red shirts, billowing sailor trousers, and wide belts with enormous brass buckles. Some had pigtails of hair hanging down their backs; others had long mustaches and bushy beards. They were armed with knives, cutlasses, and flintlock pistols.

Dominique You and Renato Beluche filled two artillery companies and began organizing a third. Baratarians lined up at the wharves to enlist in the Navy, and Commander Patterson soon had the *Carolina* and *Louisiana* fully manned. General Jackson was so impressed with the intelligence and abilities of Arsene Latour, one of Laffite's partners who had studied engineering in France, that he made him his chief engineer with the rank of major.

A day or so later, Jackson met briefly with Jean Laffite to thank him for his patriotic assistance. "We still are not certain which route the British Army will take," Jackson told him. "They may try a landing by way of Barataria Bay. I would like you to go down and inspect the routes from there."

Laffite agreed immediately, offering to make a thorough reconnaissance of the bayou country.

61

Jackson nodded with satisfaction. "But come back as soon as possible, Mr. Laffite. I shall need you here."

10
The Escape of Major Villeré

On December 18 the streets of New Orleans echoed to the roll of drums and the tramp of marching feet. Two battalions of Louisiana militia paraded smartly into the Place d'Armes, where their uniforms made a brilliant pattern of colors. General Jacques Villeré was holding a review of his troops for the benefit of General Andrew Jackson. And thanks to Jean Laffite, every man's musket on this day was fitted with a brand-new flint.

Christmas was only a week away, but the December sun shone warmly down upon the reviewing stand, and the wind off the river tugged gently at the Stars and Stripes high above the square. After the soldiers finished their drills, and drums and bugles grew silent, the crowd broke into shouts: "Long live Old Hickory! *Vive* Jackson!"

As General Jackson was leaving the stand he stopped to shake hands with General Villeré and compliment him upon the performance of his militiamen. Villeré bowed and then introduced his son, Major Gabriel Villeré.

"Ah, yes," said Jackson. "I believe your men are responsible for guarding Bayou Bienvenue, are they not, Major?"

"The bayou and our plantation canal, sir," Gabriel Villeré answered respectfully.

"Be vigilant," Jackson said and moved on to his carriage.

Two days later the general was delighted to hear that Colonel Coffee had arrived on the outskirts of New Orleans with an advance force of eight hundred Volunteers. Coffee's men went into camp on a plantation four miles north of the city, and Jackson rode out to greet them.

Compared to the well-groomed, neatly uniformed militiamen whom Jackson had become accustomed to seeing in New Orleans, the Volunteers appeared to be an unmilitary group of men. They had marched almost a hundred miles in three days, and they were in need of shaves and haircuts. They wore dingy linsey-woolsey shirts, rust-colored pantaloons, and coonskin caps. They carried long-barreled muskets and powder horns, hunting knives and tomahawks.

"A rough-looking set of men, Colonel Coffee," the general commented dryly. "Does my heart good to see them. A few hundred more like them and the British will never set foot in New Orleans."

Three thousand more arrived the next day—Colonel Billy Carroll's Tennesseans and Colonel Tom Hinds' Mississippi Dragoons. Carroll's men were mostly raw recruits, frontiersmen who knew how to use their rifles but were untrained as soldiers. While they were floating down the river, however, they had learned how to drill and fire by command on the flatboat. They had spent half their time on the oars and half at military practice.

Except for General John Thomas' Kentuckians, General Jackson now had all the men he could hope to obtain—fewer than six thousand soldiers scattered around the approaches to New Orleans. Opposing these thinly spread Americans were eight or ten thousand crack British troops who could concentrate all their power at any point they might choose.

By December 23 Andrew Jackson's impatience had turned him fretful and quick-tempered. Where were the British? None of his scouts, not even Jean Laffite, could find any trace of the king's army.

Jackson had no taste for fighting defensively. He wanted to attack, to send his best troops against the invading enemy. But he was not certain where the enemy was, and he knew that he would endanger the safety of New Orleans if he took any sizable body of soldiers out of quick reach of the city.

On that day before Christmas Eve of 1814, Royal Street was in a holiday mood, but Old Hickory was pacing around his headquarters, anxious for news of the British. Late in the evening a report came in of five British ships sighted at the west end of Lake Borgne near Bayou Bienvenue. Jackson immediately sent Major Arsene Latour, his chief engineer, with a party downriver by reconnoiter all inlets and tributaries along the east bank.

About the same time that this reconnoitering party was leaving New Orleans, Major Gabriel Villeré had just finished a horseback ride around the family's sugar plantation. Major Villeré had seen no evidence of any British patrols. The day was warm and humid, and he felt like sitting down in an easy chair on the veranda of his house. He lit a cigar and leaned back.

Through a wreath of cigar smoke, Gabriel Villeré thought he saw movement in the orange trees below the house. He stared, saw nothing more, then closed his eyes. When he opened them again the orange grove was filled with British soldiers, hundreds of them in red coats crossed with white shoulder belts. A squad was approaching him with rifles at ready. In another moment, Major Villeré was a prisoner. He replied excitedly in French to a British officer who wanted to know if any American soldiers were in the neighborhood.

When Major Villeré saw that the officer did not understand him, he continued to babble in French, pretending he understood no English. As Villeré was not in uniform, the British officer soon decided he was of no importance to him and turned away, leaving only a few men as guards.

Villeré waited patiently. When the guards became careless, he sprang to his feet and leaped through a latticework at the end of the porch. The surprised soldiers fired after him, but Gabriel Villeré was swift-footed. He darted through the shrubbery, leaped a picket fence, and charged into a cypress swamp. A few minutes later he was in a rowboat crossing the Mississippi River.

It was midafternoon when Major Villeré galloped up to 106 Royal Street on a mud-spattered horse. He dropped from the saddle and dashed inside.

General Jackson glared at the excited young man, keeping his voice calm as he asked: "What news do you bring, Major?"

66

Villeré gasped for breath. "Hundreds of British soldiers are on my plantation!" he cried. "They must have killed or captured my men guarding the bayou."

Villeré's plantation? Jackson remembered at once where it was, and his face turned pale. The British Army was less than ten miles from New Orleans!

11
In the Camp of the British

After the British defeated the American gunboats in the Battle of Lake Borgne on December 14, they chose Pea Island as a rendezvous point for their invasion force. Because of shallow waters, the troops had to be moved there by flatboats from ships in the Gulf of Mexico. For several days, boatload after boatload of soldiers landed on Pea Island.

The British brought no tents to the island, and the flimsy shelters they made of reeds gave very little protection against drenching rains and chill winds. They had no firewood, and for almost a week existed on hard crackers and strips of salted meat. It was a relief to the men when orders finally came on December 21 to begin loading in flatboats again. This time they would be going all the way to New Orleans, or so their officers told them.

In the advance brigade were the King's Own Regiment (the Fourth), the Bucks Volunteers (Eighty-fifth), the green-uniformed Ninety-fifth, a company of Congreve rocket troops, and a detachment of engineers. Many of these soldiers had fought against

Napoleon in Europe and against Americans in Maryland and Washington, D.C. No soldiers in the world were more experienced or better trained. The brigade's commander was Colonel William Thornton, who four months earlier had led the charge into Washington.

British scouts and spies had already chosen the route that Colonel Thornton's advance brigade was to follow. They would enter Bayou Bienvenue and move up it into a canal which drained the Villeré plantation. Along the east bank of the Mississippi, between Villeré's and New Orleans, was a row of sugar plantations which would make an excellent route for marching into the city.

Because of the ease with which he charged into Washington, Colonel Thornton was scornful of American soldiers. He believed the bayous and swampy ground between Lake Borgne and Villeré's would be more of a hindrance than any soldiers he might meet. Once he reached the solid ground of the sugar plantation, he was confident he could march his brigade into New Orleans as smoothly as he had entered Washington.

About midnight of December 22, Thornton's forward scouts surprised and captured a detachment of American soldiers who were guarding the entrance to Bayou Bienvenue. A few minutes later, British boats began moving up the bayou. Aboard one of them was Lieutenant George Gleig of the Eighty-fifth Regiment. He made notes of the journey: "As day dawned, a singularly wild and uninviting waste of country opened out before us. Not a tree or bush of any kind. One wide waste of reeds alone met the eye. Onwards we swept, the banks on either hand closing in upon us till first we were necessitated to contract our front, from five boats abreast to three, and finally only one."

When they entered the Villeré canal, Lieutenant Gleig noted: "We were now steering up a narrow cut. It was an admirable spot for a secret expedition, covered by reeds, so lofty as to obscure any object which could float in the canal. No eye could watch our proceedings and we too were shut out from beholding all other objects besides our own line of boats and the blue sky."

By late morning of December 23, Colonel Thornton's brigade was moving through a cypress forest, with ghostly Spanish moss hanging from the trees. Then they were in the open, looking across a field of cane stubble to the orange grove of the Villeré house. New Orleans was less than ten miles distant, with firm ground for marching all the way.

It was there that they captured Major Gabriel Villeré and then carelessly allowed him to escape. Colonel Thornton wanted to start immediately for New Orleans, but he was under orders to hold his men on the plantation until his commanding general, John Keane, arrived.

General Keane, meanwhile, had been questioning the captured American soldiers. The prisoners told him that General Jackson had at least twelve thousand men, probably more, ready to defend New Orleans.

When Keane arrived at Villeré's plantation in the afternoon, he found Colonel Thornton waiting impatiently for orders to move against New Orleans. Keane reminded the colonel that they were now in the enemy's country. "It could be disaster for us if we attack with only the first brigade," Keane said. "The

American prisoners report that Andrew Jackson has an army of several thousand soldiers."

"Several thousand rabble in dirty shirts," Colonel Thornton replied contemptuously. "My men are fresh and confident of victory."

"We can afford to wait," General Keane replied firmly. "The second brigade will be coming up during the night with more artillery. Bivouac your troops here and we will attack in full force tomorrow morning."

As soon as orders were given, the British soldiers made camp. For the first time since leaving their transport ships, they built fires to cook hot meals and dry out their clothing. Scouting parties moved out in all directions but found no traces of any American outposts. Squads were then sent to raid plantation houses and barns, bringing back many fine hams and chickens.

General Keane ordered the British flag run up to the top of a tall tree, and a regimental band played "God Save the King." After a leisurely dinner of captured plantation delicacies, Lieutenant George Gleig relaxed beside a warm campfire to note down his thoughts: "As the Americans have never yet dared to attack us, there is no great probability of their doing so on the present occasion."

12
Old Hickory Attacks

While the British were relaxing on that fateful afternoon of December 23, General Andrew Jackson in New Orleans was preparing to do exactly what Lieutenant Gleig thought he would not dare to do— attack the invading British Army. Jackson's first response to the news brought him by Major Villeré was anger. "I will smash them, so help me God!" he shouted. "By the eternal, they shall not rest on our soil!"

After a few moments, however, the general became quite calm. "Captain Reid, we must fight the British tonight. We dare not take more than half our men because the enemy troops at Villeré's may not be the main force. I want you to ready every messenger you have and send for more. First, send a courier to Colonel Carroll and put him on notice that his Tennesseans must guard the Gentilly road and the city while we go downriver. After that's done, tell the orderly to bring me a bowl of warm rice to soothe my stomach."

For the next hour the general sat at a table, dispatching orders, swallowing an occasional spoonful of rice, and studying the map which showed locations of the scattered troops that he must bring together. The place of assembly would be Montreuil plantation, just below Fort St. Charles.

He kept Captain Reid and several lieutenants racing back and forth to the mounted messengers outside: "See that two pieces of artillery are started on the road to Montreuil's at once." "Has Commander Patterson replied to my request to have his warships ready to sail before sundown?" "Find Jean Laffite." "Have my horse saddled and ready in a quarter of an hour."

About three o'clock General Jackson and Captain Reid left Royal Street and rode to Fort St. Charles where the Seventh and Forty-fourth Regulars were awaiting orders to march. Major Henry Peire was at the gate to meet them.

"You received my orders assigning you command of the Seventh Regiment, Major?" Jackson asked as he dismounted.

"Yes, General, the men are ready."

"We'll march as soon as the Volunteers and militia arrive. You may soon have a closer look at some of those Redcoats you saw in Pensacola, Major."

"The Regulars will give them a smart welcome," Peire promised and then added: "Will you come into quarters and rest, sir?"

Jackson shook his head. "No, Major, I'll wait here by the gate and greet the soldiers."

He could see Hinds' Dragoons already approaching, their horses' hooves clopping in a steady beat against the hard-packed street. Jackson ordered them to move on through the gate to the river road. "Reconnoiter cautiously below Montreuil plantation," he said to

73

Colonel Hinds, "but make no show of force if you see British patrols."

Within the next few minutes Colonel Coffee's five hundred Mounted Riflemen came cantering through, the men giving out loud cheers for Old Hickory when they recognized him standing beside the gate. Behind the Tennesseans was a company of blacks, former slaves who had been given their freedom. Then came a platoon of Choctaw Indians, a company of U.S. Marines, and a company of New Orleans lawyers and merchants, uniformed in blue hunting shirts and wide-brimmed black hats, who called themselves Beale's Rifles.

As the various units passed, Jackson occasionally motioned to an officer to drop out of ranks and join his escort troop. When he saw the Laffite brothers gallop out of a side street, he beckoned them to the gate. "I can use a pair of good smugglers," he said jestingly, "who can find their way to the British in the dark."

"Let Pierre speak for himself," Jean Laffite replied with a grin. "I await your orders, General."

Pierre Laffite dismounted and bowed politely. "I, too, sir, am at your service."

Last of all to arrive was Major Jean Plauché's battalion of dismounted militia. From Fort John on Lake Pontchartrain, these men had run at a steady jog trot all the way into New Orleans—287 proudly uniformed carabineers, dragoons and chasseurs. "Ah, here come the brave Creoles!" Jackson cried when he saw them.

He turned toward his horse. "Mount up, gentlemen," he quietly ordered his escort troop.

As the general and his escort moved along the side of the column, the pale December sun was setting. A chilly winter twilight settled over the levee road, and mists began curling off the river.

About five o'clock Jackson reached the head of the column. Colonel Coffee had halted his troops along the Rodriguez Canal facing Chalmette plantation. "Pass an order to your men, Colonel Coffee, to keep absolute silence," Jackson said. Against the misty sky he could see the glow of British campfires. "No more than two miles between us now, and the enemy suspects nothing."

Colonel Hinds came up out of the dusk. "My reconnaissance estimates two thousand British, sir."

"We match them in numbers then." He turned to Captain Reid. "Has our artillery arrived, Captain?"

"Two six-pounder fieldpieces, sir."

"Good. Send back for Colonel Denis De La Ronde to come up to me. His plantation is just ahead of us. We shall form our line there."

As soon as Colonel De La Ronde arrived, Jackson began outlining his plan of attack. "The artillery, with the Marines in support, will move along this levee road. The line, extending from right to left across the cane fields, will begin with Major Peire's Seventh Regulars, who will open the attack. On his left the Forty-fourth Regulars, next Major Plauché's Creoles, Major Daquin's Negro battalion, and Captain Jugeat's Choctaw. Colonel Coffee will command his Volunteers, Colonel Hinds' Dragoons, and Beale's Rifles in a wide sweep to the swamp side of La Ronde's plantation. There he will dismount his men, attack the British flank and rear, and roll them back on this levee. Colonel De La Ronde, you will guide Colonel Coffee over the rough ground of your back fields."

75

"I will do my best, General," De La Ronde replied. "May I also suggest Pierre Laffite as a guide? He knows my cypress swamp better than I."

Jackson laughed. "I knew we could make good use of a smuggler on such a dark night. Monsieur Pierre Laffite will report to Colonel Coffee." He turned and glanced anxiously toward the fog-covered river. "Any sign of the *Carolina* yet, Captain Reid?"

"I believe the warship is approaching, sir."

Very slowly out of the windless night, the dark shape of the *Carolina* floated alongside the levee and lowered a gangplank. The time was 6:30 P. M.

"Go aboard," Jackson said softly, "and tell Commander Patterson to open fire on the British camp one hour from now. That will be our signal to attack."

A shroud of mist whirled away, and for a minute or so a pale moon gave enough light so that the men on the levee could see the *Carolina*'s decks. The ship's guns were out and ready for firing. The Baratarians in their bandannas, wearing huge earrings and carrying cutlasses, never more resembled pirates than on that night. Jean Laffite, who was standing near General Jackson, whispered proudly, "Formidable, are they not, Old Hickory?"

"Indeed so." The gangplank lifted and the *Carolina* began sliding silently away. "Very well, gentlemen," Jackson said. "Form your regiments and battalions for the advance." He mounted his horse, pulled a blanket around his shoulders, and moved off with the artillery and the Marines.

On the field below, the men were beginning to march. The only sounds were the faint hoofbeats of Coffee's mounted troops hurrying away toward the cypress swamp and the rustle of boots against the stubble. As Jackson neared La Ronde plantation, he could see the British campfires burning brightly; then a frost-laden mist rolled in from the river and obscured them.

By 7:30 P. M., the American line was only five hundred yards from the British outposts. With orders whispered from man to man, the units came to a halt. Every soldier was alert, eyes to the front, awaiting the signal for attack.

Suddenly it came: a ball of red fire enlarging in the fog, the first gun of the *Carolina* exploding over the British camp. For good measure, Commander Patterson also fired off red, white and blue rockets. Then he opened with all his guns, their red flashes followed by booming echoes.

From his position on the levee, Jackson could hear the officers of the Seventh Regulars barking commands. By heads of companies the regiment moved off along the edge of the cane field, and the other units followed in quick succession.

The British campfires blinked out as though doused by a sudden rainstorm. For a few minutes the Redcoats seemed to be in a panic. They rushed up the levee and fired their muskets foolishly at the *Carolina*, which had anchored out of range near the western bank. The rocket company sent their fiery missiles streaking across the sky, but they fell harmlessly into the river. As soon as the British officers realized they were also being attacked by soldiers on the ground, they quickly formed a defense line and began firing volleys in return.

On the levee Jackson ordered his two cannons to begin firing into the enemy line, and the British fell back, keeping up a stubborn defense as they did so. In the darkness, however, the Seventh and Forty-fourth Regulars found themselves entangled in a rail fence and a drainage ditch. While they were trying to re-form their lines, they came under fire of the New Orleans militiamen, whose line had swung out of position.

This confusion, brought on by fog and darkness, was followed by a lull in the firing. Voices echoed weirdly. Above the shouts of angry foot soldiers came the faraway command of a gunnery officer on the *Carolina*: "Now, my lads, load again, and give those tarnal Britishers another round of grapeshot. Fire away, lads!"

Jackson smiled, but his jaws tightened when he saw the muzzle flashes of a reinforced British line charging forward again, taking advantage of the Americans' momentary holdup. He peered anxiously toward the cypress swamp on the north, wondering if Coffee's Volunteers were about ready to strike the Redcoats on their flank and rear.

A British force was closing in on the levee now, firing volley after volley, their drummers beating a steady rat-a-tat. They had brought small artillery pieces forward, concentrating fire upon the flashes of Jackson's two cannons. A rain of small shot sprayed the artillery positions. A cannon lurched forward; one of the horses was wounded. The animal reared, overturning the gun carriage.

In a flash of fire Jackson saw a line of Redcoats sweeping up the slope toward his guns. The British poured a fusillade into the Marine defenders, forcing them to give ground.

Without hesitation Jackson cocked his pistol and ran forward, shouting: "Save the guns!" The Marines rallied quickly, forming a defense ring around Old Hickory and the cannons.

In another two or three minutes the determined British soldiers might have overrun the outnumbered defenders, but a reserve company of the Seventh Regulars came rushing to the rescue and drove the British off the levee bank. When the Regulars halted to reload their muskets, Old Hickory urged them on: "Charge! Charge!" he cried. "Push on the bayonet!"

He stood up straight, staring again across the dark field toward the swamp. The misty air was so filled with powder smoke that he could barely see a faint twinkling of muzzle flashes, like hundreds of fireflies in the distance. "Captain Reid!" he cried. "Look there. Could that be John Coffee's Tennesseans?"

Reid raised his field glass. "Yes, sir! They're coming in on the British flank. In a wide front."

Jackson took the glass. After a moment he nodded with satisfaction. "Those quick-loading sharpshooters will give the British a hot time of it now."

During the next hour, Coffee's dismounted Volunteers swept through the British lines in the darkness, fighting Indian style, separating into small units and striking the Redcoats from all directions. In hand-to-hand combat they used their muskets as clubs and frightened several British soldiers into surrendering without firing a shot.

In the midst of the engagement, Colonel Coffee discovered that a fresh regiment of Redcoats had just arrived by boats and was being rushed onto the field. The reinforcements took positions behind an old levee. After several attempts to drive them into the open, Coffee decided the action was too costly and ordered his men to continue their sweep toward the river. With his staff and several British prisoners of war, Coffee made his way to General Jackson's post on the levee.

The time was now 9:30 P. M. While the disorganized and scattered units on both sides reassembled in the darkness, the firing was gradually coming to an end.

"Too much fog, too much powder smoke, too dark to tell friend from foe," Colonel Coffee grumbled. "But we did bring you some prisoners, General."

"I see." Jackson's cold eyes glared at the dark shapes of the disarmed British soldiers in the background.

"One of them is an officer, a Major Samuel Mitchell. He boasts of setting fire to our Capitol in Washington."

"He'll have little to boast of here," Jackson said harshly. He was sitting on a gun carriage, a blanket drawn close around his hunched shoulders. "Make yourself easy, Colonel Coffee. We'll just wait here for a spell. If the Redcoats have received many reinforcements, they may ask for another fight tonight."

Captain Reid had gone to question the prisoners, and Jackson could hear the murmur of voices, Reid's soft Tennessee drawl, the English officer's deep-pitched replies. Then the Englishman asked a question: "Why does your general so dislike the British?"

"During the War of the Revolution," Reid replied, "Andy Jackson was taken prisoner by one of your officers. He was only thirteen years old then, but when the British officer ordered him to black his boots, young Andy refused. So what does your arrogant British officer do? He slashes young Andy with his saber. General Jackson still carries the scars with as much pride as he hates the British for giving them to him."

80

Jackson strained to hear the Englishman's reply, but the words were indistinct. He smiled to himself, wondering how John Reid had come by that story. He'd never told it to him. Maybe he'd better set John Reid straight, he thought, about one thing. He bore no hatred for the British—except those who came to conquer the United States of America.

With a sigh the general looked out over the dark cane field where his soldiers were waiting silently in the chilly fog. Downriver the British camp was equally dark and still.

"Major Latour reporting, sir." The black-bearded Baratarian was breathing hard from the climb up the levee.

"Ah, my chief engineer," Jackson said warmly. "I had some fears you might've been captured or bogged in the swamp, Major. What's your recommendation?"

"That we withdraw the Army to Rodriguez Canal, between the Macarty and Chalmette plantations. The canal has no water in it but offers a fine defense, and the British would have to cross several ditches to get at us there."

Jackson nodded his head slowly. "I remember the ditches. To Rodriguez Canal it is, then. If they try a dawn attack, we'll be ready for them. Captain Reid! Pass the order to commanders."

By first daylight of that foggy Christmas Eve, the American soldiers had moved back two miles and were in position behind Rodriguez Canal. To keep watch on the enemy, General Jackson placed Hinds' Dragoons in front of the canal facing Chalmette plantation. He also ordered his commanders to start their men building an earthen rampart twenty yards to the rear of the canal.

81

When the fog cleared for a few minutes, Jackson could see the *Carolina* still at anchor opposite the British camp. The British soldiers were now crowded along the land side of the levee, using it as a cover against the warship's guns. Through his field glass he began examining the enemy's forward positions. There was no evidence of preparations for a morning attack, but back near the cypress swamp he could see marching soliders. Line after line of Redcoats were coming in from the boat landings. These new arrivals wore kilts and ostrich-feather bonnets. They were the Ninety-third Highlanders, and every man in the regiment was at least 6 feet tall.

13
The Americans Build a Rampart

Late in the morning of that overcast Christmas Eve, the *Louisiana* set sail from New Orleans and joined the *Carolina* opposite the British encampment. Throughout the day, whenever the Redcoats showed themselves, one or both warships would send blasts of grapeshot in their direction. In this way the British Army was kept pinned down while the Americans piled earth and mud upon their breastwork behind the Rodriguez Canal.

On Jackson's orders, Colonel Carroll brought most of his Tennessee militia down from the Gentilly road, adding several hundred more men to the diggers. Meanwhile the two 6-pounder guns were mounted behind the line, and couriers galloped off with orders to move more artillery from New Orleans to the canal.

All through the day, wagons rolled along the river road from the city, unloading spades, axes and hand-carts at the canal. For most of the morning, Jackson stayed in his saddle, riding back and forth along the line to encourage his men. His deep-set eyes were ringed with marks of weariness; he had not slept for two days, and the only food he could take was more boiled rice.

83

The Rodriguez Canal, which ran in a straight line for a mile between the levee and the cypress swamp, was 10 feet wide and 5 feet deep. Its sloping sides were overgrown with grass; its bottom was a layer of black mud. The digging crews first spaded up grass strips and carried them back 30 yards to start the base of the breastwork. Attempts to dig a trench along the earthen wall were abandoned because the ground was too soggy. General Jackson then sent details of men to bring rails from nearby plantation fences. They drove the rails into the ground while other crews cut cypress logs in the swamp, dragged them out, and placed them between the upright rails.

Not satisfied with the slow progress of his fortification, the general ordered empty barrels, sugar casks, and bales of cotton brought from barns and rolled into the line. Over all these solid objects, the diggers piled mud dug out of the deepening canal, which Jackson planned to turn into a moat by cutting a hole through the levee and letting water flow in from the Mississippi River.

For his headquarters, Jackson chose the plantation house of Augustin Macarty. It stood only a hundred yards behind the line. From a wide window on the upper floor of the Macarty house, Jackson could watch construction of the rampart, operations on the river, and activities of the enemy. The British had already moved their outposts onto Chalmette plantation.

In the afternoon, Major Latour came up to make a report on his efforts to engineer a cut through the levee. "Unfortunately, sir, the level of the Mississippi is falling. Unless the river rises, we cannot flood the canal."

84

"Then we'll fill it with crowfeet spikes. They can be hauled out from New Orleans before dark. The men can also cut sharpened stakes and angle them toward the enemy position."

"You do not plan to attack again, General?" Latour asked.

"No, Major. Our little Christmas fandango last night was necessary and accomplished its purpose. Had we not attacked last night, the British would be marching into New Orleans today and we would be fighting for our lives." He turned and looked out the window toward Chalmette plantation. "Now they're off balance, uncertain of what we'll do. But the safety of the city of New Orleans depends entirely upon our little army out there building that mud wall. We can't risk defeat by attacking in the open again."

Latour stepped to the window, his hands clasped behind his back. "Yes, we could use more men behind that rampart."

"I have hopes that General Thomas will arrive with his Kentucky militia before the British make their move. Since we can't be certain of the Kentuckians' arrival, however, I have another task for you, Major."

"Yes, sir?"

Jackson turned to his map on the table. "I want you to begin construction of two more breastworks between here and New Orleans—for us to fall back upon if necessary. You will choose the proper sites."

Latour looked puzzled. "Where do we obtain men to perform the labor, sir?"

"New Orleans is under martial law," Jackson replied harshly. "We shall conscript able-bodied citizens to do the work."

After Latour left, the general noticed that the mist had turned to rain, blown by a chill wind from the Gulf. If his men must endure bad weather, then he too would endure it. He put on his outer coat and tramped down the stairway. "Major Reid," he said as he went out, "the troops will need dry blankets tonight. Send a courier to New Orleans for them. Confiscate, if necessary."

The Christmas Eve twilight came early in the drizzle, but the soldiers kept working. Old Hickory stayed with them, riding back and forth, stopping often to praise them for their steadfastness. By nightfall they were placing crowfeet spikes and sharp-pointed poles in the Rodriguez Canal. The mile-long rampart was now four feet high, but the men were determined to double its height before morning. They counted off in alternate ranks, to take turns sleeping and digging to Christmas Day.

14
General Pakenham Arrives

On Christmas morning, mists still lay over the cane fields. Suddenly from the British camp came the boom of a cannon. Before the echoes of the explosion rolled away, another roar followed. Along the rampart behind Rodriguez Canal, the mud-encrusted American soldiers dropped their spades and rushed for their muskets. Bugles sounded alarms, officers shouted commands, and men began falling into ranks.

Out on the level plain between the canal and Chalmette plantation, a platoon of Hinds' Dragoons galloped toward the British outposts. The horsemen wheeled and came trotting back toward the canal.

General Jackson rode out to meet them. "Where are they directing their fire?" he cried.

One of the dragoons shouted back: "It's not an attack, sir! The British are saluting a general just arrived by boat."

The new British commander was Major General Sir Edward Michael Pakenham. Surrounded by a staff of a dozen officers in resplendent scarlet and white uniforms, General Pakenham strode from the boat landing and gripped the hand of General Keane.

"Welcome, sir," General Keane said. "A good voyage from England, I trust?"

"Other than the storm which delayed us," Pakenham replied. He removed his large cocked hat and mopped his brow with a silk handkerchief. Pakenham was a young general, his cheeks smooth and ruddy, his keen blue eyes dancing with curiosity as he studied the British encampment.

"Commanding officer's quarters have been prepared for you in the plantation house yonder," General Keane said.

"Later," Pakenham answered curtly. "I wish to inspect my forces first, General. A riding horse?"

"I'll have one brought from the barns, sir."

"I shall go and select one myself. I hear these American planters have fine riding stock."

As they continued toward the orange grove Pakenham said pointedly: "I expected John Keane would have been in New Orleans by Christmas Day."

General Keane's face turned red. "The backwoods rabble under Andrew Jackson chose to make a fight of it. In my judgment we must build a strong force here before marching into the city."

"Quite so." Pakenham smiled, his blue eyes dancing again.

On his horseback ride around the British lines, Pakenham asked many questions of General Keane but seldom bothered to comment upon Keane's replies. He also asked questions of young line officers he met along the way. One of these was Lieutenant George Gleig, who had been wounded in the neck during the night battle of December 23 and was still wearing a bandage.

"How did you receive your wound, Lieutenant?"

"Bayonet, sir."

"Close fighters, these backwoods Americans, eh?"

"They have no knowledge of how war should be fought," Gleig replied indignantly. "Why, sir, they attack our outposts at night and pick off our sentinels. They sneak up silent as Indians and then all fire at once. In Europe when we fought the French, our sentinels were sometimes no more than twenty yards apart, with gentlemen's agreement not to molest the other." Lieutenant Gleig sighed. "But these American savages, they have no chivalry."

"Trifling obstacles, Lieutenant," Pakenham said, "compared with those so often opposed by British valor. Be assured, our occupation of New Orleans is certain."

From the secondary line, Pakenham had a chance to see the "savages" who so annoyed Lieutenant Gleig. A squadron of Hinds' Dragoons came galloping across the cane stubble, whooping like Indians, taking quick shots at the British outposts, and then swinging out of range of return fire.

"They do yell like the wild natives of this country," Pakenham said. As he was turning away a shell from one of the American warships burst over the British camp, sending officers and men scurrying for cover.

Pakenham sat calmly in his saddle, but his face darkened with anger. "Why have the American warships not been sunk to the river bottom, General Keane?"

"Our light fieldpieces cannot reach them, sir," Keane explained. "I have ordered twenty-four-pounders to be brought from our ships, but the guns have not arrived."

Pakenham shook his head indignantly. "We cannot tolerate this shelling of our base. We must silence those two watery dragons out there at once." He stared across the river at the *Carolina* and the *Louisiana*. "Call all staff officers to a council of war at my headquarters, General."

In the well-furnished drawing room of Major Villeré's captured plantation house, Major General Sir Edward Michael Pakenham sipped from a glass of the sugar planter's best rum. He was listening to reports from his officers. He seemed impatient of their explanations concerning the surprise night attack and the various reasons given for not pursuing the Americans into New Orleans.

"With the forces at our disposal, gentlemen," he interrupted, "our entrance into New Orleans should have been swift and easy. I regret the defeat of our forces due to the error made on the twenty-third of December. Our troops should have advanced to New Orleans immediately on taking Villeré's plantation. However, that is past. Let us look to our present position. I do not like it. So long as the two American warships remain in the clear to shell us as they please, we cannot properly assemble our regiments for the march into New Orleans. I am asking Admiral Cochrane to assign crews of his stoutest sailors to hasten the movement of guns from our ships so that we may blow the American warships from the water."

When he paused, there was a chorus of approving ayes from the officers present.

"The American ships lie about a mile away, and I do

90

not expect they can be silenced by piercing their hulls at that distance. So we shall treat them to hot shot and set them on fire. In addition to heavy fieldpieces, I shall want at least two howitzers, one mortar, and as many furnaces for heating cannonballs as the artillery commander expects can be put to use."

He glanced at Admiral Cochrane who nodded agreement. "While this necessary operation is in progress," Pakenham added, "we shall continue to increase our forces here. In the coming hours, regiments of the East Essex and the Royal North British Fusileers will be arriving." His blue eyes twinkled. "Gentlemen, let us be patient for another day or two. The rich prize of New Orleans is well worth the waiting."

15
Bombardment of the Warships

On the morning after Christmas, Jean Laffite arrived at the Macarty plantation house and was directed up the stairway to General Jackson's quarters. "You sent for me, sir?" the tall Baratarian asked.

"Come in, Mr. Laffite." Jackson turned his chair away from the window. "I suppose you have heard that the British are bringing up heavier artillery?"

"Some of my swamp observers reported this, sir."

"Yes. Well, now, that means we must do the same. We have two twenty-four-pounders at Fort St. John on Pontchartrain, under command of Dominique You and Renato Beluche. How long would it take your Baratarians to bring those guns down here and mount them on our rampart?"

Laffite smiled. "I hear Dominique is furious because we left him back at the fort and away from the action. If I give him the word they'll transport the twenty-four-pounders down here, mount them, and have them ready to fire by nightfall."

Jackson showed his satisfaction with a brisk nod.

"You may pass the word to Dominique You by one of my mounted messengers, Mr. Laffite."

"General Jackson, may I offer another suggestion concerning our defenses?"

"Certainly."

"The rampart ends in a straight line at the cypress swamp. Because of the soft earth there, the wall has sunk badly. And because the swamp is shallow at this season, the enemy could wade through the woods for several hundred yards beyond the end of our line."

Jackson picked up his spyglass and swung around to the window. "In other words, the British could turn our flank there," he said almost in a whisper. "What do you propose?"

"That we cut logs, anchor them to the trees, and build barricades upon them above the waterline."

"Well spoken, sir!" Jackson cried. "Mr. Laffite, I thank God you are on our side and not with the British. My engineers will begin the work at once."

"At your service, General." Laffite bowed. "I shall start the messenger to Dominique, who will be much pleased to join us here."

Later in the day, Jackson received a report from Colonel Hinds. His dragoons had observed the British at work on the levee. They were mounting a battery of heavy guns overlooking the river. As soon as the general read the report, he told Captain Reid to inform Commander Patterson that his warships were in danger. "Suggest that he move them out of range before daylight," Jackson added.

But at first daylight of December 27, while Jackson was still getting into his uniform, a heavy gun blast

93

rattled the windows of his room. A moment later, Captain Reid knocked on the door. "A message, sir, from Commander Patterson. For lack of a breeze, they have been unable to sail the ships upriver!" Another roar of artillery drowned out the captain's words.

Jackson fixed his spyglass on the *Carolina*. Smoke was pouring from a hole near the stern of the vessel. "The British gunners are using hot shot! Captain, order some men into light boats—the Baratarians are there at the levee—they're good oarsmen—send them speeding across to the *Louisiana*. I fear it's too late to save the *Carolina*, but we must save the *Louisiana* and her guns!" The captain was already gone, racing down the stairway.

Through his spyglass the general could see sailors leaping off the decks of the *Carolina*. Flames shot up into the ship's rigging. The masts began to totter, falling with showers of brilliant sparks into the river. Another British cannonball crashed into the powder magazine. The *Carolina* blew up, throwing flaming fragments into the sky and shaking the windows of the Macarty house.

Shifting his glass to the *Louisiana*, Jackson watched anxiously as the ship's crew threw out ropes, launched boats, and began towing her out of range. Under a hail of hot shot that sent geysers steaming from the surface of the river, the Baratarians from the shore joined the ship's crew. They rowed like madmen, but the *Louisiana* seemed barely to move. A shell tore across her decks, but that was the only direct hit. The other firings fell short, farther and farther behind, and then suddenly all the American soldiers along the rampart began cheering. The *Louisiana* had been saved.

Suspecting that the British must be ready to begin a

ground attack, General Jackson now ordered Hinds' Dragoons to blow up the buildings on Chalmette plantation. "The buildings block our field of fire," he explained. "If we do not destroy them, the British will use them as shields for their artillery and troops."

Although the British strengthened their outposts during the afternoon, they made no attack. Jackson decided that they were waiting for the next morning. To keep them on edge for lack of sleep, he ordered squads of snipers to take turns approaching the British lines and harassing them through the night with unexpected fire.

December 28 dawned bright and clear with frost sparkling on the cane stubble in front of Rodriguez Canal. From his observation window, Old Hickory watched Dominique You and his red-shirted Baratarians trotting up to their gun battery. Their two 24-pounders were solidly emplaced in the rampart, with cotton bales stacked around them. The men set to work swabbing and charging the cannons.

Suddenly, out of the sky streaked hundreds of hissing rockets, the British Army's new terror weapon. They had used these Congreve rockets against American troops at Lundy's Lane and in the bombardment of Fort McHenry. General Jackson's frontiersmen had heard about them; now they were being attacked by them.

Like wild meteors the rockets streaked through the air, smoking and sputtering over the rampart and the Macarty house. Their charges exploded with terrific blasts of sound. When they struck the ground, their fifteen-foot shafts, with pointed iron heads, writhed through the cane stubble like angry snakes.

Old Hickory dashed outside, mounted his horse, and

galloped along the defense line. "Pay no attention to the rockets, boys! They are mere toys to amuse children!"

Meanwhile, the British artillery had opened fire. Some pieces were aimed at the mud rampart, others at the *Louisiana* offshore in the river.

A few minutes later two separate columns of British infantry began marching out from their camp. One column was near the levee, the other near the swamp, with a line of green-uniformed skirmishers between them. General Jackson held his reins for a moment, frowning at the compact formations. The scarlet and green colors of the enemy uniforms were bright in the morning light. To a monotonous drumbeat, the British troops came steadily closer, arms and legs swinging like controlled clockwork, as though nothing on earth could stop them from their purpose.

16
Artillery Duel

"Hold your fire!" Old Hickory shouted. The command, repeated by officers, echoed along the rampart. The British column marching near the levee was now only five hundred yards away. In rigid ranks, shoulder to shoulder, staring straight in front, the Redcoats moved closer and closer. Behind the rampart, a line of American riflemen stood ready. At the five artillery batteries, gunners eagerly awaited commands to fire.

Jackson turned his horse, facing the *Louisiana*. What was Commander Patterson waiting for? A moment later, flashes of fire darted along the starboard side of the warship. Patterson's gunners had opened with a salvo.

The first British formations fell apart before the blasts of shot. But they closed ranks quickly, marching steadily onward, ignoring their casualties. Another burst from the *Louisiana* tore into them, and this time the column wavered. British officers on horseback galloped forward, shouting commands, and the tight formations became files, the men spreading out so as to offer less compact targets.

Now the American batteries on the rampart opened up, spewing grapeshot across the field. The skirmishers and the British files went down like falling dominoes. Before they could recover, the *Louisiana* joined in with raking fire along the British flank. The Redcoats took cover in shallow ditches.

Across the cane field, the British column marching along the edge of the swamp was having better luck. While the American artillery was concentrating on the column near the river, the Redcoats moved in close enough to threaten the end of Jackson's defense line. Jean Laffite's floating rampart was not yet finished, and the low embankment offered little protection to the American troops there. In an attempt to slow the enemy's advance, Colonel Billy Carroll sent detachments of his Tennessee militia and a company of Choctaw Indians splashing off into the swamp to strike at the British flank.

Out of the moss-draped cypress woods, the Tennesseans and the Choctaw poured volleys of musket fire, but the well-trained British infantrymen refused to panic. With parade-ground precision they changed fronts and closed with their attackers. Both sides exchanged musket fire at close range, and then the outnumbered Americans faded back into the swamp. British officers were giving commands to move on against the rampart when a mounted messenger came galloping up from Pakenham's command post. Pakenham's order was to withdraw to the nearest ditches until more British artillery could be brought up to protect the infantry.

After a few minutes, Pakenham's horse-drawn fieldpieces came bouncing across the cane stubble. The artillerymen moved them expertly behind what cover they could find—low mounds of earth, tree stumps, and the remains of the Chalmette buildings. They opened fire, but the cannons along the rampart and aboard the *Louisiana* immediately replied. The battle had become an artillery duel.

Dominique You's Baratarians now had their furnace in operation. They heated their shot to a red glow and then aimed them at the wrecked plantation buildings. When the planks began burning, the Baratarians blasted them into blazing fagots that sent British artillerymen and infantrymen diving into the nearest ditches. For several hours the duel continued until every British cannon in range was knocked out of operation.

This was enough for General Pakenham. He ordered his troops to file to the rear in small squads, but when the Redcoats sprang out of the ditches where they had taken cover, American artillerymen sprayed them with grapeshot. The column near the swamp retreated in good order, but the Redcoats beside the levee ran helter-skelter for the rear. Along the rampart, American riflemen fired off farewell salutes, laughing and jeering at the fleeing soldiers of the king's army.

Old Hickory, however, was not yet ready to celebrate a victory. He knew that General Pakenham had only been testing the Americans with a reconnaissance in force. Pakenham would try again, perhaps somewhere else, perhaps with many more soldiers and guns next time.

For the following three days Jackson drove his men at a furious pace, building up the rampart with more logs and cotton bales. He ordered Jean Laffite's floating

99

platform extended in a long arc into the swamp and had cotton bales placed upon it. Any British column attempting to swing around the end of the rampart could now be trapped in deadly enfilading fire.

Jackson also worried about the *Louisiana.* If the British somehow found a way to sink his only remaining warship, half of his artillery would be at the bottom of the river. After conferring with Commander Patterson, he decided to remove one 24-pounder and two 12-pounders from the ship and form them into a battery on the levee across the river. Even from that distance, the guns could rake the flanks of any British infantry attack. He also brought seven more cannons from New Orleans, placing them along the rampart.

From his observation post in the Macarty house, General Jackson could see that Pakenham was also building up his artillery power. The Redcoats worked through the nights, constructing log barricades and bringing field guns as close as seven hundred yards to the Rodriguez Canal.

To hinder these enemy preparations, Old Hickory risked the safety of the *Louisiana* by sending it silently downriver every night. The warship fired broadsides at the emplacements, then quickly turned about and sailed out of range of the British guns. Jackson also organized parties of night raiders to carry 6-pounder guns close to the enemy outposts. Sudden explosions from these small cannons kept the British awake through the last nights of December.

The last day of 1814 was piercing cold, with occasional drizzles of rain, but Old Hickory announced that the American Army would celebrate New Year's Day with a formal review. He arranged for a band to be brought out from New Orleans and ordered a tall flagstaff mounted in the center of the rampart. At first dawn of the new year of 1815, the British would see the Stars and Stripes flying defiantly in the breeze.

17
Rocket Attack

In the British camp that last night of the year, General Pakenham's soldiers worked unceasingly. They were under orders to complete the artillery batteries for a New Year's Day attack upon the American defense line.

During the day, British sailors had brought up several more naval guns from Lake Borgne. These heavy weapons had to be emplaced upon platforms shielded by mounds of earth. As added protection, barrels of sugar were rolled out of plantation warehouses and stacked around the guns.

Although the night was pitch-black, with a cold drizzle falling, the British placed eighteen cannons in fortified positions before daylight. Immediately behind the guns, rocket troops constructed six batteries of Congreve rocket launching tubes.

Pakenham's battle plan for New Year's Day was to open with a furious rocket and artillery bombardment against the American gun positions, knock them out quickly, and blast holes in the rampart. After this would come a rushing infantry attack which was expected to storm through the breaks in the line.

So determined was Pakenham to have everything complete by morning, he ordered junior officers to join enlisted men in work details. Lieutenant George Gleig had to take his turn with a pickax and spade while his platoon built up mounds of earth around one of the batteries. Lieutenant Gleig complained of a shortage of rations; he had only one sea biscuit and a bite of salt beef. To satisfy his hunger, he nibbled at brown sugar from the confiscated barrels.

At first dawn, fog was so thick that Lieutenant Gleig could not see the American line. But he could hear drums and trumpets sounding reveille, and a few minutes later he heard military music coming from behind the rampart. "The airs which they played were some of them spiritless enough," the lieutenant noted belittlingly. "The Yankees are not famous for their good taste in anything, but one or two of the waltzes struck me as being peculiarly beautiful. The tune, however, which seemed to please themselves the most was their national air known by the title of 'Yankee Doodle.' They repeated it at least six times in the course of their practice."

About nine o'clock the fog lifted suddenly as if a curtain were rising to reveal a stage. Lieutenant Gleig was amazed to see American soldiers in smart marching formations behind the rampart. The bands continued to play, flags and pennants were flying, and American officers in dress uniforms were riding about on horses. The Americans were staging a formal review right under the big guns of the British!

Apparently the Americans were equally surprised at what the rising curtain of fog revealed to them in the British camp. The parade broke up quickly, the soldiers rushing to their positions along the rampart.

At the same time, Pakenham's command post signaled the rocket troops to begin firing. A stream of rockets whistled across the field, and the heavy guns then opened with a thunderous roar that shook the earth. The first rockets lifted high over the rampart, doing no damage but leaving clouds of black smoke in their wakes. The second volley hit squarely on targets—the cotton bales around the American batteries—and set some of them on fire. Again the big guns roared, concentrating fire on the same cotton bales.

By this time the American gunners were ready to reply. Puffs of smoke billowed from the rampart batteries. And then from the cover of a drainage ditch, Lieutenant Gleig was horrified to see the effects of the first bombardment upon the battery he had helped construct during the night. American cannonballs plowed through the mud embankment, penetrated the sugar barrels, and knocked a field gun out of position. Two gunners went down.

"Ammunition! Ammunition!" a British artillery officer was shouting. "Ammunition to the front!"

18
"The Watchword Is 'Fight On!' "

When the British opened their artillery attack on New Year's morning, General Jackson and his staff officers were on the porch of the Macarty house. They were watching the troops assemble for review. Suddenly rockets and cannon shot peppered the roof and upper walls, sending bricks and splinters flying. Window glass crashed to the ground.

Old Hickory rose calmly, buckling on his sword. He was pleased at how quickly his troops were responding to the attack. With muskets in hand, they fell out of formations to dash to their assigned positions along the rampart. Another shower of shot rattled against the Macarty house.

"Well, Captain Reid," the general said dryly, "this place is too dangerous for us. Let us join our soldiers on the front line." Disregarding the exploding rockets overhead, he led the way across the muddy field.

At Battery No. 3, Dominique You and Renato Beluche were sighting their cannon barrels on the nearest British batteries. Dominique raised up to shake his fist at the Redcoats, condemning them in a mixture of French and English oaths for spoiling the parade and stopping the band music. A shell burst overhead, and a piece of metal ripped red shirting from Dominique's sleeve, burning his arm. He swore loudly in pain and anger. Again he shook his fist. "I'll make them pay for that!" he shouted and motioned to a pig-tailed Baratarian to apply a burning match to the fuse.

With a loud explosion, the shell screamed across the canal, tearing into a British battery—a direct hit. "This time we cram the gun to the mouth with chain shot and canister!" Dominique cried. "We will wrap the Redcoat gunners around their cannon!"

Meanwhile, Renato Beluche's crew was firing. They, too, scored a hit, knocking a big gun to pieces.

But the British gunners also were finding their targets. Cotton bales around the American batteries were being torn apart by shells, and Congreve rockets were setting them afire. Not far from where Old Hickory was standing, a rocket streaked into a caisson filled with ammunition, blowing it up with a mighty roar.

Captain Reid reacted by jumping in front of the general to shield him from flying shot. Black smoke boiled over the rampart, so it was impossible to see or breathe. Old Hickory coughed and hurried on along the line.

At the next battery soldiers were pushing bales of burning cotton into a muddy ditch below. Others poured water on ripped bales that were beginning to blaze.

As soon as he reached a place that was clear of smoke, Jackson raised his spyglass to survey the field. "I count five of their artillery pieces disabled," he said

106

to Captain Reid. Beyond the smoke of the British guns, he could also see their infantry massed near the levee, awaiting a command to attack the rampart. Over by the cypress swamp three platoons of British sharpshooters, most of them in the green uniforms of the Ninety-fifth Regiment, were marching cautiously along the woods line. As he watched them, they began disappearing into the trees.

Old Hickory shifted his glass back to the end of the rampart. He grunted with satisfaction when he saw a company of Colonel Coffee's Tennesseans filing out into the swamp. They splashed knee-deep into the water and mud, holding their long rifles high.

A few minutes later, small-arms fire was crackling between artillery bursts. The British sharpshooters emerged from the woods line, their leggings black with swamp mud, and began retreating. "John Coffee's boys were ready for them," Jackson said.

Less than an hour after the British bombardment began, thirteen of their cannons were disabled and out of action. Their only infantry thrust had been driven back. By midday all firing had ceased. For the third time since their advance brigade reached Villeré's plantation on December 23, the discouraged Redcoats turned around and marched back to their camp.

Old Hickory spent the early part of the afternoon walking back and forth along the rampart, praising his troops and counting the costs of the British attack. Eleven of his men had been killed, 23 wounded. Three artillery pieces were badly damaged, two caissons destroyed. The burned and mangled barricades of cotton bales would have to be rebuilt. But the defense line had held firm, and its accurate gunners had wrecked most of the enemy's forward artillery.

Later in the day Jackson returned to the Macarty house, where soldiers were busily shoring up the damaged walls and supports. "Captain Reid," he said, "write out a New Year's message to the troops. Tell them the commanding general sends them his good wishes for a Happy New Year, and especially to the officers and men at the pieces of artillery. Tell them the watchword is 'Fight On!'"

19
The Kentuckians Arrive

For the next two days the American troops worked at repairing their damaged rampart and artillery pieces. Old Hickory strode back and forth along the line, glaring out across the flat cane fields, wondering what the British would try next. His scouts and spies were unable to get close enough to General Pakenham's camp to obtain much information of value. Jean Laffite's swamp observers reported that the Redcoats were bringing up many small boats and that they were gathering sugarcane stalks into several large heaps on La Ronde plantation.

On January 4, a welcome visitor arrived at the Macarty house. He was Colonel John Adair, and with him was a company of the long-expected Kentucky militia. Adair explained that General John Thomas, commander of the Kentuckians, was so ill that he had been left under care of a doctor in New Orleans. "The rest of our troops are strung out for miles up the Mississippi on keelboats and rafts," he said, "but they should all be here in another day."

"How many Kaintucks volunteered?" Jackson asked.

"More than two thousand."

"Well done!" Old Hickory's eyes shone with pleasure. "I have always held Kentucky riflemen in high esteem, Colonel Adair. Now that you and your men are arriving, I am sure we have an edge on our British enemies."

"As soon as my men are issued arms, sir, they will be ready for battle."

"Issued arms?" Jackson frowned. "Do your Kaintucks not have their long rifles?"

Colonel Adair shook his head. "Less than a thousand of them brought arms from Kentucky."

"I don't believe it!" Old Hickory shouted. "I've never seen a Kentuckian without a gun in my life."

Colonel Adair smiled, but his face quickly turned serious again. "Kentucky was almost swept clean of weapons to fight the British along the Great Lakes. But my men are willing to fight with their hunting knives."

"Yes, I'm certain of that." Jackson turned and called for Captain Reid. "Captain, we must find more than a thousand firearms for the Kentuckians. If necessary we'll take them from the New Orleans guards."

"The guards are armed with old Spanish muskets, sir. Worn out and rusty."

"Order them to be turned in and brought down here at once. If they can be made to fire, the Kaintucks will know how to do it. And now, Colonel Adair, as your men arrive, have them make camp in the field behind our lines. I will inspect them tomorrow."

Next day when Old Hickory rode out to the Kentuckians' camp, he was pleased to see so many brawny, determined-looking frontiersmen. Except for a troop of rangers in green buckskins, however, the men had no

110

uniforms. Coats and trousers were threadbare, many having holes at knees or elbows. "Your men need warmer clothing, Colonel Adair," Jackson declared. "I shall call on the good ladies of New Orleans to sacrifice their blankets. They can cut them into pantaloons and cloaks for these brave men of Kentucky."

On January 6, Jean Laffite brought fresh reports from his Baratarian spies. Several hundred more British reinforcements were coming in by boats from Lake Borgne. The British were also building small redoubts between La Ronde and Chalmette plantations. Behind these breastworks they were stacking piles of cane stalks. They also appeared to be digging in the levee near their camp.

It was the digging that worried Jackson most of all. He asked Commander Patterson to sail the *Louisiana* as close to the British camp as he dared. "Take a sharp look through your spyglass and see what the rascals are about," Jackson said.

A few hours later, Commander Patterson reported that the Redcoats had cut a hole through the levee and were collecting many small boats at the river entrance.

Old Hickory was certain now that General Pakenham was planning a river crossing. Yet he could not believe that the main attack force would cross the river for a march along the west bank and a second crossing into New Orleans. More likely it would be a diversionary force meant to capture the artillery battery across the river or to draw off American soldiers from the rampart. Old Hickory fretted and fumed through the day, spending hours at his upper window squinting at the distant British camp through his spyglass.

By a stroke of luck, the dragoons captured a prisoner that evening and hustled him promptly to Jackson's headquarters. The Redcoat's uniform was mud-stained; his hands were chafed and sore; and he was hungry. He seemed glad to be a prisoner and was willing to talk.

Jackson questioned him closely. The British camp had received more troops just arrived from England, the soldier said—General John Lambert's brigade, the Royal English Fusileers and the Forty-third Highlanders. Pakenham now had about 8,000 men against the 4,000 Americans along Rodriguez Canal.

The captured Redcoat also explained what the British were doing with the piles of sugarcane stalks. They were fastening them into fascines and gabions (bundles and cylinders). When the next attack began, each British infantryman would carry one to the Rodriguez Canal and drop it in so that following waves of infantry could cross over the spike defenses. They also had made scaling ladders, the British soldier said, but he did not know when the attack would begin.

After studying the bits of information he had obtained about Pakenham's activities, Old Hickory decided that the British general would soon throw his main army against the rampart. Pakenham apparently was willing to sacrifice the first ranks of his infantry in order to storm the line.

Yet General Jackson expected that Pakenham would also send one or two regiments across the river. Therefore, early on January 7, he ordered 500 Kentuckians to march around through New Orleans and join about 500 Louisiana militiamen under General David Morgan on the west bank. This small and poorly armed force was all that could be spared to defend the artillery battery and the western approaches to New Orleans.

All through January 7, there was much stirring about in the British camp. After watching enemy activities through his spyglass, General Jackson was convinced that an attack would come in a few more hours. Late in the day he ordered Hinds' Dragoons to withdraw to the rear of the swamp line. From their new position, these horse soldiers could pounce upon any British units that might try to sweep around through the swamp during the night.

As darkness fell, orders went out from the Macarty house to all commanders: *An enemy attack is expected before morning. One-half the men will remain awake and at battle posts through the night.*

After telling Captain Reid to awaken him soon after midnight, Old Hickory went to bed early. As he fell asleep he could hear a distant hammering on Chalmette plantation. The British were rebuilding their artillery positions.

20
Old Hickory Is Ready

At one o'clock on the morning of January 8, 1815, General Andrew Jackson was out on the rampart. The night was cold and clammy, and the men had built tiny fires behind the wall. At each battle post, the general stopped for a few minutes to talk with his soldiers.

When he reached Battery No. 3, he found the Baratarians crouched around a coffeepot on a mound of red coals. The fragrant odor of coffee filled the damp air. "That smells like better coffee than we get at headquarters," Jackson said gruffly. Dominique You arose slowly, pushing his cap back, the glow of coals lighting his grinning face. "Did you smuggle it, Captain Dominique?" Jackson asked.

"Maybe so, General, maybe so." The former pirate filled a steaming cup and offered it to Old Hickory.

Warmed by the rich coffee, Jackson felt much better. As he walked on with Captain Reid, he said softly: "I wish I had five hundred Dominiques on the parapets."

A few minutes later he was greeting Colonel Billy Carroll's Tennesseans. He called many of them by their first names, for he had known these men since their boyhoods.

By the time he reached the swamp line, the sky was beginning to turn lighter. In the drifting fog he could see outlines of mossy cypress trees. John Coffee's Volunteers stood up along the log walkway, saluting him as he passed, then sat down again to finish their breakfasts of cold cornbread. In the swamp it was impossible to keep fires going.

At Battery No. 8, near the end of the line, he found Colonel Adair waiting for him. Adair requested permission to bring his Kentuckians nearer the rampart. "Very well," Jackson replied. "Bring your men up, Colonel. If General Pakenham is a shrewd fighter, he'll hit us hardest at this end of the line. Form your Kentuckians in two ranks—those with the better rifles in front, as support for Carroll and Coffee."

Not long afterward, pickets who had been stationed out in the Chalmette cane fields began hurrying back across Rodriguez Canal. They reported that masses of British infantry were forming in wide columns on both sides of the plantation, about a half mile from the rampart.

Jackson turned to the nearest parapet and climbed quickly to the top, Captain Reid following close behind. Dawn was just beginning to break, but a bank of drifting fog screened Chalmette plantation.

Old Hickory raised his spyglass. A moment later, from the levee side of the field, a Congreve rocket streaked upward, bursting in a shower of blue stars.

"That is their signal for advance, I believe," Jackson said calmly.

And then the fog broke into patches against a pale-blue sky. Across the frost-silvered cane field marched the British—a vast expanse of red and white and green uniforms. They were advancing in two massive columns, sixty men across, coming on at a regular march step to the beat of their drums. Then they began cheering at the top of their voices.

21
The Battle of New Orleans

General Jackson saw that the British column marching along the edge of the swamp was twice as long as the one along the levee. He knew then that his Tennessee and Kentucky boys would have to bear the brunt of Pakenham's attack.

Light from the brightening sky glinted off a thousand bristling bayonets. And out on the river, small boats filled with Redcoats were crossing to the west bank.

Most of the American rifles would fire accurately to four hundred yards, and the enemy on the field was approaching that distance now. All along the rampart officers began shouting orders. "Pick out your targets," a husky-voiced Kentuckian called out. "Aim above the plates of their white crossbelts!"

Suddenly there was confusion in the British column near the swamp. Files of infantrymen began peeling off from the advance formation. They ran back and forth to low earthen breastworks, each man picking up a scaling ladder or a fascine of cane stalks. In the midst of this activity, American artillery opened fire, the British guns responding immediately. Smoke rolled over the field, adding to the confusion in the forward ranks of the Redcoats. Many infantrymen who were carrying the heavy bundles threw them down in order to ready their muskets for firing. Stragglers scattered across the frosted cane stubble.

Now all the big guns on both sides were roaring. From the rampart the artillerymen fired blasts of grapeshot. From the battery across the river, round shot hurtled into the British line along the levee. Shells furrowed the British ranks, the infantrymen dropping as though clubbed down. Lines buckled, then bunched up, only to be mowed down by grapeshot. While some American cannons fired on the marching infantry, others began knocking out the British batteries as they had done on New Year's Day.

Yet the stubborn Redcoats kept pushing forward, ever closer to the canal. A scattering of musket fire rattled along the rampart. And then, suddenly, from behind the American line, the New Orleans band began playing "Yankee Doodle." A loud burst of cheering echoed down the line.

Black smoke from the American batteries hung over the rampart and began drifting out in a thick curtain to screen the approaching British columns. The enemy infantry was now too close for the American cannon elevations. Old Hickory turned and shouted to Captain Reid: "Go down and order Batteries Seven and Eight to cease firing! Our riflemen can't see through this confounded smoke!"

As soon as the batteries stopped firing, wind whisked the smoke away. The Redcoat line was within three hundred yards, coming on the run. Along the rampart

118

the first line of Tennesseans had already primed and loaded their rifles. Commands echoed sharply: "Make ready! Aim!" Firelocks were cocked, rifle butts pressed against shoulders, fingers touched the triggers. "Fire!"

As quickly as the men in the first rank fired, they stepped back to reload, and a second rank moved up to the parapets. Commands came faster now, and the second rank was replaced by a third. From the edge of the swamp all the way across to the levee, the brisk crackle of rifles became a continuous rolling fire. For several minutes sheets of orange flame rippled along the rampart, pouring a hail of lead into the onrushing Redcoats, cutting them down in waves.

General Samuel Gibbs was in command of the British column near the swamp. Just as his forward regiment, the Forty-fourth East Essex, made a rush for the Rodriguez Canal, its first platoons were cut to pieces. The few survivors dashed for cover in the swamp. Panic spread to the rear, and the whole regiment began to break apart.

General Gibbs spurred his horse forward, attempting to rally the regiment. He waved his sword and shouted angrily at his fleeing soldiers. Because Gibbs was on horseback, the American artillerymen knew he must be a high-ranking officer. They turned their barrels in his direction, and cannon shot plowed the ground all around him, but Gibbs continued to rally his men.

Near the levee, General John Keane could see that Gibbs was in trouble. Keane knew that if Gibbs' attack failed, the battle would be lost. Without waiting for orders from General Pakenham, Keane detached his best regiment, the Ninety-third Highlanders, and started them in an oblique march across the field to aid Gibbs.

Nine hundred 6-foot Highlanders moved out in long strides, their leather bonnets aslant, their green Sutherland kilts swinging to the rhythm of their bagpipes. Cannon fire from the battery across the river raked the length of their column. The Highlanders kept marching, eyes to the front, stumbling over their dead and wounded. General Keane, who was mounted, drew a heavy fire. He was shot off his horse and had to be carried unconscious from the field.

As soon as the Highlanders came within range of the Tennessee and Kentucky positions, the frontiersmen began picking off the enemy officers. In a confusion of shouted orders the forward company came to a halt, forcing the others to a standstill. The bewildered Highlanders waited for a command, but there was no one to give it. For two or three minutes they stood stiffly at attention while the American riflemen showered them with lead. When it was over only 160 of the 900 brave Highlanders who had started across the field were still standing.

General Pakenham, watching anxiously from his post in the rear, now saw that disaster was threatening his army. He mounted his horse and dashed to the front to join General Gibbs. "The troops will not obey me!" Gibbs cried as Pakenham came up. "They will not follow me!"

Pakenham lifted his cocked hat, shouted to the scattered infantrymen to follow him, and spurred his horse forward. A burst of grapeshot exploded overhead, wounding him in the left arm and killing his horse. Pakenham's aide swung his horse over to pick up the general. Ordering the aide to dismount, Pakenham quickly took his place in the saddle. Again the British commander started forward.

This time a rifle bullet slammed into his neck and he fell to the ground. A moment later cannon shot shattered his leg. His men carried him off the field. Pakenham was dying, but before losing consciousness, he sent an urgent order to General Lambert, who was waiting with two thousand reserve troops in the rear of Chalmette plantation: "Bring up the reserves!"

Meanwhile, General Gibbs had galloped ahead to take Pakenham's place with the rallying troops. The infantrymen made a dash for the canal, but again the American rifle fire mowed them down. Gibbs was hit three times; his horse was shot from under him; but he kept charging on foot. He was only twenty yards from the Rodriguez Canal when a fourth bullet struck him dead.

In a foolhardy display of courage, Major Thomas Wilkinson raced forward to take General Gibbs' place. Wilkinson led 100 soldiers through the spiked defenses of the canal, and he and about 20 men lived to reach the smoke-clouded rampart. None of them carried scaling ladders. All except the major huddled close to the wall to keep out of the line of fire. But Wilkinson forced himself up the slippery parapet, reaching the top, only to fall dying into the arms of a Kentucky militiaman. His men surrendered as prisoners.

Across the field Colonel Robert Rennie, who had been left in command of General Keane's column, was leading a charge along the levee. The American battery across the river blasted into his column, but the British soldiers fought their way up to a bastion of cotton bales at the river's edge.

With Rennie was young Lieutenant George Gleig. In the midst of the booming guns and rattling rifles, Gleig was surprised to hear the American band playing "Yankee Doodle."

Sword in hand, Colonel Rennie leaped upon the platform, ordering the American riflemen to cease firing. "The enemy's works are ours!" he cried. A moment later a platoon of blue-shirted New Orleans militiamen, Beale's Rifles, came storming up from their line position. Colonel Rennie was the first to fall, and then in a hail of bullets all his men were driven off the bastion. Lieutenant Gleig was trying to climb the parapet when he was shot in the head; he fell back and lost consciousness.

No mounted British officers were now left on the battlefield. Pakenham, Gibbs and Rennie were dead or dying. Keane was unconscious from his wounds. Only one British general was left to command—John Lambert. He was still holding his two thousand reserves in readiness for attack. By the time a messenger reached Lambert with Pakenham's order to bring up the reserves, the battlefield was covered with hundreds of British casualties.

Although Lambert feared that the battle was already lost, he moved his reserves forward. All that he could do was to slow the retreat of the beaten British regiments. Lambert saw now that it would be madness to order another attack on the American defense line. He sent messengers across the river, calling back the small force which had crossed in boats, and ordered his officers to prepare for a retreat through the swamps to

122

the British warships. He would ask General Andrew Jackson for a truce to gather up the dead and wounded.

At 8:30 A. M. the battle was ended. With the last rattle of rifle fire, the New Orleans band began playing "Hail Columbia." American soldiers along the rampart stared with astonishment at a battlefield which only an hour or so earlier had been covered with white frost. Now it was covered with the scarlet and green uniforms of hundreds of British dead and wounded.

Then, as though by some silent command, dozens of British soldiers slowly rose all around the field until there were five hundred of them. They had survived by falling and pretending to be casualties. They dropped their weapons and came forward to surrender.

General Jackson now called his staff together to discuss pursuit of the British Army. Colonel Hinds wanted to drive what was left of the enemy back into the Gulf of Mexico, but most of the other commanders were against any more fighting. They believed the British were beaten and would never again try to take New Orleans.

Agreeing that a pursuit would only lose American lives and gain nothing, Old Hickory decided to hold fast at the rampart. But he ordered the artillery to keep up a long-range fire to discourage the British from returning.

Early in the afternoon a mounted messenger carrying a flag of truce came riding out of the ruins of Chalmette plantation. The British commander requested permission to remove casualties from the field. Jackson granted a suspension of arms for two hours and offered the assistance of his troops in burying the British dead.

When the artillery ceased firing, an awesome silence fell over the plantations along the river. Platoons of

American soldiers moved out cautiously from the rampart and began helping the British soldiers gather up dead and wounded. After the count was completed, the British found they had suffered 1,971 casualties. The Americans had lost only 7 killed and 6 wounded.

Among the British wounded was Lieutenant George Gleig, who had been carried to the rear by his comrades. When he recovered consciousness, he was told that the British were retreating to their ships. Being a loyal Englishman, Lieutenant Gleig was dismayed to learn that his king's army had been defeated.

What Lieutenant Gleig did not know—and no one else in America would know for another month—was that the slaughter of January 8 should have never happened. On Christmas Eve, or two weeks before the great battle, American and British diplomats met at Ghent and signed a treaty of peace ending the War of 1812. Ghent was in Belgium, however, and the news had to come by sailing ships across the Atlantic Ocean. General Jackson did not learn of the war's end until February.

Although the battle need not have been fought, it convinced the British that the young nation which called itself the United States of America would fiercely defend itself against invasion. The battle also proved to eastern Americans that western Americans were loyal fights for the Union, and thus it helped unite East with West.

The Battle of New Orleans made a hero of General Andrew Jackson, the first frontiersman to become a national hero. A few weeks after the victory, new songs were being sung about him: "The Battle of New Orleans," "The Eighth of January," "Old Hickory."

General Jackson's favorite was a ballad that the Kentucky boys sang as they marched back home over the Natchez Trace:

> I suppose you've read it in the prints
>   How Pakenham attempted
> To make Old Hickory Jackson wince,
>   But soon his schemes repented;
> For we, with rifles ready cocked,
>   Thought such occasion lucky,
> And soon around the general flocked
>   The hunters of Kentucky:
>   O! Kentucky,
>   The hunters of Kentucky.
>
> Old Hickory was wide awake
>   And wasn't scared at trifles
> For well he knew what aim we take
>   With our Kentucky rifles;
> So, he led us down to Cypress Swamp,
>   The ground was low and mucky;
> There stood John Bull in martial pomp—
>   But here was Old Kentucky:
>   O! Kentucky,
>   The hunters of Kentucky.

Soon the whole nation was singing that song. Its echoes followed Andrew Jackson down the years to 1828, when the people elected him President of the United States.

Index

126

Forty-fourth Regulars, 35
Forty-third Highlanders, 112

Ghent, Treaty of, 124
Gibbs, Samuel, 119
Gleig, George, 69-71, 72 ff., 88-89, 103-4, 122, 124
Gordon, John, 17-18, 38
Grand Terre Island, 27, 32, 61
Great Britain: invasion of United States, 16-19; Battle of Fort Bowyer, 20-26; in Florida, 35-37; Battle of Pensacola, 38-45; Battle of Lake Borgne, 51 ff.; Battle of New Orleans, 117-25. *See also* British

Hermes, HMS, 22 ff.
Hinds, Thomas, 55, 64, 93, 123
Hinds' Dragoons, 87, 89
Horseshoe Bend, Battle of, 7-15
Houston, Sam, 11-13

Jackson, Andrew, 25-26, 32; and Battle of Horseshoe Bend, 7-15; march to Florida, 33 ff.; Battle of Pensacola, 38-45; in New Orleans, 46-50; and Jean Laffite, 57-62; attacks British, 72-82, 83-86, 87-92, 92-96, 97-101, 102-4, 105-8, 109-13, 114-16; Battle of New Orleans, 117-24
Jackson's Tennesseans, 11, 16
Jones, Thomas Catesby, 48-50, 51 ff.

Keane, John, 70-71, 88-90
Kentuckians, 55-65, 109-11, 119-20
King's Own Regiment, 68

Laffite, Alexander, 58. *See also* You, Dominique

Laffite, Jean, 27-32, 50, 52, 57-62, 63, 73, 76, 92-93, 98-99, 111
Laffite, Pierre, 30-31, 34, 76
Lambert, John, 112, 122
La Ronde plantation, 109
Latour, Arsene, 61, 65, 81, 84-86
Laval, William, 25-26, 39-40
Lawrence, William, 18-19, 20-26
Lockyer, Nicholas, 27 ff., 52-53
Louisiana, USS, 49, 61, 83, 90, 94, 96, 97-100, 111

Macarty, Augustin, 84
Macarty plantation, 81, 92, 113
Madison, James, 19
Manrique, Don Matteo, 17, 41-42
McWilliams, Captain, 27 ff.
Mercier, Lieutenant, 33-35
Mississippi Dragoons, 36, 64, 73
Mitchell, Samuel, 80
Mobile, 18-19, 20 ff., 25, 33, 46-47
Montreuil plantation, 73
Morgan, David, 112
Mounted Riflemen, 74

Napoleon, 16
Natchez Trace, 55
New Orleans, 18, 29-32, 34-35, 46-50, 63; Battle of, 117-25
Nicholls, Edward, 18, 21-22, 29
Ninety-fifth Regiment, 68
Ninty-third Highlanders, 82

Orleans Dragoons, 33

Pakenham, Edward Michael, 87-91, 98-99, 102-4, 115, 117 ff.
Pass Christian, 51-52
Patterson, Daniel, 48, 52, 54, 61, 73, 76-77, 94, 97, 111
Pea Island, 68
Peire, Henry, 36-37, 44, 73
Pensacola, 16 ff.; Battle of, 38-45
Pensacola Bay, 35

127

The Author

DEE BROWN is the author of numerous books, including the widely acclaimed best-selling *Bury My Heart at Wounded Knee.* A native of Louisiana, Mr. Brown is a librarian on the staff of the University of Illinois Library. He was a printer and a reporter before he became a librarian and began to write books. He and his wife have two children and live in Urbana. His most recent book for Putnam's was *Showdown at Little Big Horn.*